# A WRITER'S GUIDE TO WASHINGTON

Isolde Chapin
Publication Director

Thomazine Shanahan
Editor

Joel Makower
Managing Editor

WASHINGTON INDEPENDENT WRITERS

Typesetting by Rings-Leighton Ltd.
Printed in the United States of America by
Bookcrafters Inc., Fredericksburg, Virginia

ISBN 0-912521-00-7
Library of Congress Catalog Card Number 83-50044

First Printing, June 1983

Published by

Washington Independent Writers
525 National Press Building
Washington, D.C. 20045

# Contents

# Acknowledgments

Producing this book, the first major publishing venture under-taken by Washington Independent Writers, has called on the talents and stamina of many of its members. The idea, originated by staff, was first proposed to WIW's 1981-1982 Board of Directors by Luree Miller, Chair of the Publications Committee. With Thomazine Shanahan serving as editor and Joel Makower assuming the role of managing editor, the WIW 1982-1983 Board accepted a detailed proposal to fund the publication of the *Guide*.

WIW President Dan E. Moldea, 1981-1982, provided the early support to the project that got it underway. Review of the manuscript was entrusted to two former presidents of WIW, Paul A. Dickson, 1979-1980, and Joseph Foote, 1980-1981, and to former WIW Executive Director Judith Brody Saks. Current WIW President Daniel Rapoport, 1982-1983, gave editorial staff a free hand, but was always there to assist on questions and problems.

Michael J. Whelan, Chair of the 1982-1983 Publications Committee, contributed financial and budget know-how to this project. Ronald Schechter, Esq., of Goldfarb, Singer & Austern worked on a pro bono basis from start to final review of the manuscript, counseling on the many legal steps along the way.

A number of WIW specialists read sections of the manuscript to supply scope where necessary and to concentrate on accuracy: Ruth Darmstadter, Jeffrey P. Davidson, Sara Ebenreck, Sara Gilbert, Tim Kennedy, Patricia L. Moore, and Theresa Ward Warner. Luree Miller, Chris and Gene Rosenfeld, and Rosemary Beavers assisted beyond measure in matters of substance and detail.

The book's cover and chapter headings, with their feel for Washington's traditional cherry blossoms and fireworks, were designed by artist Tom Thill.

Word processing of the manuscript was performed, with a writer's sensibilities, by WIW member Gigi Pickford Barse.

Betty Scheewe and Joan McKee of National Advertising Service turned out mounds of photocopies of successive drafts of the *Guide* to meet each deadline. Patricia Spellman proofread galleys.

The writers—WIW members all—wrote and rewrote. They located the resources. They are the book.

There was a great deal of cooperation as well as many a crisis. The rough edges and editorial complexities of all sorts were smoothed away by Kitty Stone, Assistant to the Director of WIW.

Everyone close to writing and producing *A Writer's Guide to Washington* has found it a massive endeavor. But even during discouraging moments, the idea of creating a book specially targeted to the needs of writers in a city where writing is a major industry never failed to rekindle enthusiasm.

*—Isolde Chapin*
*Executive Director*
*Washington Independent Writers*

# Introduction

Washington is full of writers, men and women who make their living by the pen (or by the typewriter or the word processor). Some write for newspapers or magazines. Some write for the government. Some write for associations or for businesses. And some write books and poetry. Many write part-time—as a supplement to another job or to raising a family. And there are consultants, lobbyists, academics, and researchers galore, all of whom make writing a part of their lives in Washington.

*A Writer's Guide to Washington* is meant for all of them.

The writer, in Washington as elsewhere, of necessity wears many hats. In addition to conducting research and specializing in a subject area, writers often act as their own employment bureaus as well—constantly seeking new assignments, exploring new markets. And the independent writer—one who freelances—always acts as entrepreneur. Keeping in mind that balancing of roles the writer must perform helped us to delineate the areas we wanted to cover in this book. *A Writer's Guide* is therefore divided into four sections: "The Writer as Researcher," "The Writer as Specialist," "The Writer as Entrepreneur," and "The Writer at Leisure."

Statistics are elusive. Washington's press corps is generally counted as 3,000 strong. Washington Independent Writers lists nearly 1,400 members. The story goes that the government's hiring arm, the Office of Personnel Management, is swamped with applicants for writer and editor slots. However you measure it, writing as a profession thrives in Washington.

Signs of the writing life proliferate. Three major organizations devoted to writers and to writing have emerged over the past decade: WIW, now nearly ten years old; The Writer's Center, in its seventh year; and the newest, the local chapter of the Writer's Union. These three join with the National Press Club, the Washington Press Club, and various other writers' institutions, many of which are described elsewhere in this book. Conferences and courses devoted to every imaginable aspect of writing abound in the metropolitan area. Universities here have on their staffs writers of the first magnitude, among them novelist Susan Shreve at George Mason University, poet Roland Flint at Georgetown University, and critic-novelist Doris Grumbach at American University. The prestigious PEN/Faulkner Award For Fiction has recently moved its office to the Folger Shakespeare Library on Capitol Hill.

This book reflects the writer's presence in the federal city. It offers a guide to the resources, the tools, and the services of special interest to those who write for a living or for pleasure. We hope that *A Writer's Guide to Washington* will be useful to those outside the writing profession, too. Students of all ages will find it helpful, as will visitors to the region. And for all those of any profession who simply love this city, we hope to provide a new insight, a new information source, or simply a new place to sit and enjoy the view.

*—Thomazine Shanahan*
*Editor*

# The Writer
# As Researcher

Gathering information precedes nearly every act of writing. The Washington writer finds a wealth of material to choose from; this section attempts to survey and to illuminate those sources most basic to the researcher. "The Federal Government" looks at Congress, the White House, the judicial branch, and the executive agencies, examining the people and the resources unique to each. Special subsections on the "Defense Department" and on "International Resources" provide writers with tools to penetrate the complex military establishment, and to survey an array of organizations and representatives ranging from embassies to the World Bank. "Lobbying" examines the presence of the private sector in Washington and its role in attempting to influence the government. Both the government and the lobbying chapters provide case studies that illustrate the practical application of the information presented. "Libraries and Archives" covers the formidable range of institutions open to writers here, including the Library of Congress, the National Archives, and a host of others. "Photo Files" clarifies the complex process of locating and crediting the illustrations that accompany a writer's words.

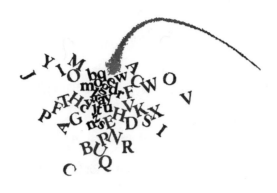

# The Federal Government

## Steve Weinberg

Finding your way through the Washington bureaucracy is easier than it looks. Although the federal government looms as a vast repository of facts, statistics, and reports—and the people who produce them—there is order within its labyrinth. After cracking the code—discovering which people to talk to and which documents to pursue—the job becomes simpler.

The more sophisticated the approach, the more the Washington of Congress and the White House, the Cabinet departments and the special agencies, the lobbyists and the diplomats, will serve as the tools of the trade.

Consider the potential sources. The federal government employs more than 2.8 million civilians, plus another 2.1 million in uniform; they are spread throughout the 50 states and most foreign countries, but the largest concentration is in Washington. On Capitol Hill alone, nearly 18,000 government employees work, and each one is a potential source. The Pentagon in suburban Virginia is the workplace for so many that their names take up

---

*Steve Weinberg is a freelance writer and journalism professor in Washington, D.C.* Trade Secrets of Washington Journalists *is his most recent book.*

nearly 200 pages of small print in that building's telephone directory. The international scene lends a measure of glamor and enrichment to Washington's cultural life. Most sources are American, but Washington does offer the opportunity to be in touch with the world.

The federal government is kept afloat by documents. The executive agencies send nearly 3,000 required reports to Congress every year. In addition, the agencies generate thousands more reports on a one-time basis. Congress not only receives those reports, but produces thousands of documents itself every year, not to mention a seemingly endless number of bills. Cases in the federal courts add millions more pages, most of them open to writers who know where to look.

## Congress

Contacting members of Congress is frequently the best way to begin a story; other times, trying to talk to them makes little sense. Of course, senators, representatives, and their staffs are generally good sources for stories on politics. They are sometimes good sources for stories about specific issues, as well, especially if that issue falls in the domain of a congressional committee on which the member serves.

When is a member of Congress most likely to talk willingly with a writer? If a story is related to the home district, or to an issue being debated by his or her committee, the chances of access increase. Access is also enhanced when you represent a publication that will bring desired visibility to the member of Congress, or when you have a personal reference from a mutual acquaintance. Members of Congress, however, pursue hectic schedules, and it's often best to try catching them immediately before or after a hearing relevant to the issue, or, frequently, by phoning directly for an interview.

Staff members, however, are often the most useful and most available sources for writers. They normally fall into one of three categories—personal staff, committee staff, or support staff.

In a congressional office, personal staff usually includes caseworkers, who handle constituent questions and complaints that arrive among the tens of thousands of letters every month; secretaries, who keep the appointment books; legislative correspondents, who answer queries about public policy; legislative assistants, who keep members of Congress informed about issues being considered in Congress and serve as liaisons with committees, where most policy is shaped; the administrative assistant, who is attuned to politics and often is the member of Congress' alter ego; and the press secretary, who deals with writers.

Personal staff can assist in a number of ways. They know their boss' predilections, both personal and legislative. They know how national issues affect voters back home. They can obtain documents from nonpublic sources and pass them along. They can explain the politics behind the public debate.

Committee staff in the House and Senate differ from personal staff in some important ways. The staff of a committee tends to be made up of issue specialists with professional backgrounds; lawyers and economists are more likely to be on committee staffs than in personal offices. Each committee and subcommittee has jurisdiction over specific issues, although there is considerable overlap. For example, some 83 committees and subcommittees deal with energy issues in the House alone; in the Senate, energy matters are under the jurisdiction of a mere 18 committees and subcommittees. In some committees, the members of Congress and the staff tend to be bi-partisan—Republican-Democratic or conservative-liberal differences mean little. Other committees are partisan indeed. Sometimes writers can play majority staff against minority staff to obtain information. When researching any topic, you should determine which committees have jurisdiction, then interview the majority and minority staff members who know the most.

In addition to personal and committee staff, members of Congress are served by support staff. This staff may be divided roughly into issue specialists and administrative support.

Congress has specialists concentrated in its four offices that conduct studies on numerous topics—the General Accounting Office, Congressional Research Service, Office of Technology Assessment, and Congressional Budget Office. These specialists tend to be career employees with no obvious political allegiances. They are almost always helpful to writers, although their first priority is to assist members and their staffs.

Other issue specialists are available in the caucuses and political party groups of Congress. The caucuses—such as the

## Congressional Telephone Numbers

Congressional Switchboard . . . . . . . . . . . . . . . . . . 202/224-3121
Democratic House Floor Action . . . . . . . . . . . . . . 202/225-7400
Republican House Floor Action . . . . . . . . . . . . . . 202/225-7430
Legislative Status Office . . . . . . . . . . . . . . . . . . . 202/225-1772
Upcoming House Floor Schedule, Democratic . . . 202/225-1600
Upcoming House Floor Schedule, Republican . . . 202/225-2020
Upcoming Senate Floor Schedule, Democratic . . . 202/224-8541
Upcoming Senate Floor Schedule, Republican . . . 202/224-8601

Congressional Women's Caucus, the Congressional Black Caucus, and the Environmental and Energy Study Conference—are formed by members of Congress, who pay staff to research issues within the caucus' domain. The political party groups employing issue specialists include the Democratic Study Group and the Republican Conference, both in the House of Representatives.

Other congressional resources include the offices of the Clerk of the House and Secretary of the Senate. They can assist writers trying to unearth expenditures by a member of Congress, disclosure forms showing a member's personal wealth, and the like.

Finding people on Capitol Hill is easy. Their offices are in the Capitol Building itself or in office buildings within walking distance of the Capitol. All members of Congress and most of their personal staffs have space in the Longworth, Cannon, or Rayburn buildings (House) or the Russell, Dirksen, or Hart buildings (Senate). Committee staffs are in the Capitol, one of the six office buildings just named, or in a nearby annex building. The same is true of the administrative support staffs and some of the issue specialists, including the caucuses and the Congressional Budget Office. The Congressional Research Service is located within the Library of Congress buildings; the General Accounting Office and Office of Technology Assessment are in buildings several blocks away.

Both House and Senate phone directories are useful for the writer on the Hill. The House phone book is compiled by the

Clerk of the House. The Senate book is compiled by the Senate Sergeant at Arms. You may reach these and any other congressional offices by dialing the main switchboard for Congress, 202/224-3121; operators are consistently helpful, 24 hours a day, seven days a week.

Capitol Hill staff members, like their employers, are busy people. Walk-ins without appointments are rarely greeted with delight, so phone ahead for appointments. It's helpful to have a phone location where you may be reached for call-backs. (See page 116 for information on telephone answering services and equipment.)

To learn more about elected members of Congress other than their office locations and telephone numbers, you may consult numerous sources. Brief biographies are in the *Congressional Directory,* published every other year by the Congressional Joint Committee on Printing and sold by the Government Printing Office. Nongovernmental publications with detailed information about individual members of Congress include *Politics in America* (Washington, D.C.: Congressional Quarterly Press) and the *Almanac of American Politics* (Washington, D.C.: Government Research Corporation). Two weekly magazines sometimes run profiles of members—*Congressional Quarterly Weekly Report* and *National Journal.* For an aggregate look at Congress, consult *Vital Statistics on Congress* (Washington, D.C.: American Enterprise Institute for Public Policy Research).

Learning about congressional staff members is more difficult. Probably the best source of biographical information is the *Congressional Staff Directory* (Mount Vernon, Virginia: Congressional Staff Directory). Political Profiles Inc., a Washington, D.C. company, issues regular biographical reports, some of which include high-ranking congressional committee staff members.

## The White House

In general, White House staff is less accessible than congressional staff. But when you make connections, White House staff members are every bit as helpful. For purposes of gathering information, White House staff may be divided into three groups—political operatives, issue experts, and administrative specialists.

The political operatives have titles such as chief of staff,

# Your Tax Dollars At Work

The federal bureaucracy is so vast that aggregate numbers might intimidate a writer. Here are some examples, meant to reduce the government to manageable proportions:

**Human Nutrition Information Service,** part of the U.S. Department of Agriculture. Room 367 Federal Building, 6505 Belcrest Road, Hyattsville, MD 20782; 301/436-8618. Provides information about healthy food.

**National Technical Information Service,** part of the U.S. Department of Commerce. 5285 Port Royal Road, Springfield, VA 22161; 703/487-4600. Central source for the public sale of government-sponsored research, plus foreign technical reports prepared by national and local agencies, their contractors or grantees. The collection exceeds 1.3 million titles.

**Patent and Trademark Office,** part of the U.S. Department of Commerce. 2021 Jefferson Davis Highway, Arlington, VA 20231; 703/557-3158. This agency issues about 70,000 patents every year and registers more than 30,000 trademarks.

**Bureau of the Census,** part of the U.S. Department of Commerce. Headquarters at Silver Hill and Suitland Roads in Suitland, MD 20233; 301/763-4051. Statistical heaven.

**Defense Contract Audit Agency,** part of the U.S. Department of Defense. Building 4, Cameron Station, Alexandria, VA 22314; 202/274-7281. Heard of cost overruns? This part of the Defense Department is supposed to help head them off. The agency evaluates the costs claimed by government contractors.

**Energy Information Administration,** part of the U.S. Department of Energy. Forrestal Building, Independence Avenue, SW, Washington, DC 20585; 202/252-8800. The source of timely reports on oil imports, natural gas supplies, and the status of other fuel stocks.

**Food and Drug Administration,** part of the U.S. Department of Health and Human Services. 5600 Fishers Lane, Rockville, MD 20857; 301/443-4177. The agency is supposed to protect Americans against impure and unsafe foods, drugs, and cosmetics. Information is available on specific products.

**Bureau of Land Management,** part of the U.S. Department of the Interior. Interior Department building, 18th and E Streets, NW, Washington, DC 20240; 202/343-5717. Responsible for overseeing nearly 350 million acres of public lands throughout the country.

**Drug Enforcement Administration,** part of the U.S. Department of Justice. 1405 I Street, NW, Washington, DC 20530; 202/633-1249. Every part of the United States has a problem with illegal drugs. This agency combats illegal drug use.

**Bureau of Labor Statistics,** part of the U.S. Department of Labor. 441 G Street, NW, Washington, DC 20212; 202/523-1913. Collects data on unemployment, wages, unions, workplace safety.

**National Highway Traffic Safety Administration,** part of the U.S. Department of Transportation. 400 7th Street, SW, Washington, DC 20590; 202/426-1828. The agency promotes safety on the highways of America. As part of that mission, it tries to determine which cars are most dangerous, which cars are costliest to repair, and which cars get good gas mileage.

**Consumer Product Safety Commission,** an independent agency. 1111 18th Street, NW, Washington, DC 20207; 202/634-7740. Conducts research to determine hazardous products.

**Federal Communications Commission,** an independent agency. 1919 M Street, NW, Washington, DC 20554; 202/254-7674. Want to know about the ownership and programming of local television and radio stations? Here is where to start.

**Federal Emergency Management Agency,** an independent agency. 500 C Street, SW, Washington, DC 20472; 202/287-0330. If there is a natural, man-made, or nuclear emergency anywhere in America, this agency is supposed to know what has happened and what the federal government is doing about it.

**Pension Benefit Guaranty Corporation,** an independent organization. 2020 K Street, NW, Washington, DC 20006; 202/254-4817. A lot of pension plans never pay off. This outfit is supposed to help workers if their pension plan fails.

*—Steve Weinberg*

counselor to the president, or press secretary. They often play a role in development of public policy, but their overriding concern is selling the president's program. Their main value for writers is their ability to explain the administration's political direction.

Issue experts are found in such White House organizations as the National Security Council, Council of Economic Advisers, Office of Science and Technology Policy, Office of U.S. Trade Representative, Office of Policy Development, and Office of Management and Budget.

Administrative specialists are employed in the White House Visitors Office, the Office of Special Presidential Messages, and the like. A writer trying to do a piece about White House tours or about how the White House handles congratulations to citizens reaching age 80 or beyond will profit by talking to these staff people.

The vice president of the United States and the first lady have their own staffs, including press secretaries.

White House staff is located in one of several buildings—the White House itself, the Old and New Executive Office Buildings, the Winder Building, and various townhouses on Jackson Place. All are within easy walking distance of one another. Anyone wishing to enter the White House or the Old or New Executive Office Buildings must have an appointment.

As with Congress, a telephone directory is helpful. The main White House switchboard number is 202/456-1414. A loose-leaf directory for the Executive Office of the President is compiled and updated regularly. It is available from the publications unit of the Executive Office. The *National Journal* publishes a *White House Phone List*, and selected telephone numbers are in the front sections of two pocket-size booklets available from private corporations. One is the *Directory of Key Government Personnel*, compiled by the Washington branch of Hill and Knowlton, a public relations firm. The other is the *Directory of Public Information Contacts*, available from the Bendix Corporation Aerospace-Electronics Group in Arlington, Virginia.

Detailed biographical information about White House officials is difficult to find in one place, except for the president and his top aides. Special editions of the *National Journal* and occasional reports from Political Profiles Inc. are two sources of information about middle-level White House staff. Another is the *Federal Staff Directory*, published by the Congressional Staff Directory Company in Mount Vernon, Virginia.

## The Executive Agencies

Thirteen Cabinet departments, 64 additional agencies, and hundreds of more-or-less autonomous subdivisions within these units are listed in the *United States Government Manual*, an official government publication updated annually. It is difficult to generalize about personnel in such an array of agencies. Yet you may penetrate the bureaucracy by remembering some common elements. For example, all agencies contain presidential appointees requiring Senate confirmation, other high-level political appointees, advisory committee members and outside consultants. All agencies also contain career personnel with similar jobs—public affairs specialists, statisticians, budget officers, liaisons to Congress, investigators trying to determine waste and fraud, lawyers who bring or defend lawsuits involving the agency, administrative law judges, and others.

Each of these people can help. Some are experts on the issues; others are not, but can lead you to the most knowledgeable source.

Many agencies have multiple office buildings in Washington and regional offices throughout the nation. The *United States Government Manual* is the best place to start.

There is no single place to find out who these people are and what they know the most about. An agency telephone directory is often the most logical starting point. Combined with the *Government Manual* and the *Federal Staff Directory*, the phone directories should be even more useful. Also check the agency's public information or press office. Advisory committee members—usually outsiders—may be located through each agency, or through the Committee Management Secretariat in the National Archives and Records Service. Outside consultants sign contracts with agencies, and those contracts are usually a matter of public record somewhere in each agency.

Presidential appointees must reveal a lot about themselves to the Senate committees that confirm them. High-ranking appointees and civil servants are supposed to file annual financial

# Defense Department

Overall military policy and strategy are developed in the Department of Defense (DOD). Weapon systems are conceived here, and their development monitored from inception through budget hearings, contracting, manufacturing, testing, and deployment. DOD handles recruiting, training, deployment, and retirement of officers and enlisted personnel. DOD is also a giant archive of written and printed material, photographs, motion picture film, audio and video tapes, and art works of various military involvements.

Countless specialists are available for consultation. Fields include legislative affairs, patents, finance, engineering, psychological sciences, environmental sciences, research, manpower, medicine, and scores of others. Specialists can be found in weapons new and old; from the MX missile to the Springfield rifle, from the F-18 fighter plane to Civil War uniforms.

In addition to obtaining information, DOD is where one makes arrangements to go aboard ship, sit in the cockpit of an F-16, interview a VIP, or visit an overseas base.

You may well blanch at the thought of tackling this vast organization. For starters, the Pentagon has 23,000 employees laboring in the largest office building in the world. An educated guess is that there are at least 200,000 telephone extensions in the building. So, where to start?

**The DOD Telephone Directory.** The key to the puzzle is a publication available for $8 at stores selling books of the U.S. Government Printing Office. Although the Directory has almost 200 pages listing the individuals working in DOD, the section called the Organizational Index is the writer's best friend. The index divides DOD into four departments: DOD itself, Army, Navy (including Marine Corps), and Air Force.

The idea behind the index is to present DOD in terms of functions rather than as individuals. This system is helpful because individuals come and go, but offices are relatively permanent.

The first move is to decide which of the four departments to contact. In general, for data on a topic that affects all the military—such as pay and allowances—DOD is the target. Data on the A-10 aircraft, however, would best come from the Air Force.

It's best not to try and puzzle out which office within a department to contact. The public affairs officer is the person to see. He or she, in turn, will either provide the information you want from files or supply the name of a specific office to contact.

A letter is usually preferable to a telephone call. It isn't easily lost or forgotten, and can be passed down the chain without change or distortion in the original request. Whether you phone or write, always identify yourself and explain why you want certain information. The more specific you are, the easier it is to get assistance. You may be asked to submit a manuscript of your book or article or a script of your proposed film or videotape.

**Freedom of Information Act.** Applying for a document under the Freedom of Information Act can accomplish two things. If a document is classified and thus not available, it might be declassified as a result of the review that your request will trigger. Or, if a document is unavailable because extensive research is needed to locate it, the FOI office may agree to search for it—for a fee. There are hourly search fees and per-page copying fees. Ask for an estimate of charges before giving the go-ahead. However, if you can convince the FOI people that your project is in the public interest, they may waive charges.

Note that the FOIA deals with individual *documents,* so you must be able to name what you want with reasonable accuracy. The FOI people don't answer questions or give opinions.

There is an FOI office in the Pentagon, listed in the DOD section, that serves all the military departments.

Charges for digging out information for you may be levied by offices other than the FOI agency. Be sure to ask before going ahead.

**Outside Military Sources.** There are a number of important sources of military information outside DOD proper. These include National Archives and Records Service, Library of Congress, and the Smithsonian Institution, including the National Air and Space Museum and the Paul E. Garber Facility in Suitland, Maryland, where military airplanes are rebuilt and displayed.

—*Spencer Bostwick*

---

*Spencer Bostwick, recently retired from Headquarters' Staff, U.S. Air Force (civilian), has had 18 years' experience writing and producing audio-visual and TV programs for all branches of the military.*

disclosure forms with their employer, just like members of Congress and some congressional and White House staff members.

## The Courts

Judges at the various federal courts in Washington rarely talk to writers. But support staff at the courts will often take time to show writers the necessary legal documents. Many writers mistakenly think only of the U.S. Supreme Court when they think of courts in Washington. However, the U.S. Court of Appeals and the U.S. District Court in Washington also handle nationally significant cases regularly. Half a dozen specialized courts—such as Tax Court and the Court of Military Appeals—hear cases that can be the grist for good stories. The Administrative Office of the United States Courts and the Federal Judicial Center employ experts on judicial policy and procedure.

The *United States Government Manual* contains basic information about each court and a main address and telephone number. The general telephone directory for the District of Columbia lists the office numbers for many individual judges.

## Documents in the Public Sector

**Congressional Documents.** Most valuable documents generated by Congress are by-products of the legislative process, so writers who fail to understand that process should brush up. A good place to begin is with the pamphlet *How Our Laws Are Made*, published by Congress itself. The pamphlet contains reproductions of the cover page of most documents published by the House or Senate.

Documents usually are available in one or more of three places—from an individual member of Congress, the appropriate House or Senate committee, or the House or Senate documents rooms. The House Document Room, in the Capitol, can be reached by calling 202/225-3456. The Senate Document Room, in the Hart Building, can be reached by calling 202/224-7860.

The first document in the legislative process is a bill, sponsored by one or more House or Senate members. All bills introduced in either chamber are mentioned in the *Congressional Record*, published each day that Congress is meeting and occasionally when Congress is in recess. You may obtain a subscription to the *Congressional Record* or individual copies from the Government Printing Office. Most libraries subscribe to it.

Bills are referred to the proper House or Senate committees after introduction. There most of them die. But some are scheduled for hearings. To learn about hearings in advance, a writer may call the committee, scan *The Congressional Monitor* (published by Congressional Quarterly Inc.), check the *Congressional Record*, or look for a listing that day in *The Washington Post*. The hearing generates the next document, a transcript of the testimony along with supporting material. Some hearings are unrelated to any specific bill; these are called oversight hearings, intended to determine how well an existing program works. Transcripts of oversight hearings are published, too, sometimes accompanied by a committee document containing findings and recommendations. However, transcripts may not be available for several months after a hearing takes place.

To learn whether Congress has held hearings on any issue, you can call the committee and hope whoever answers has a good memory. Or you can search an index published by Congressional Information Service Inc., Bethesda, Maryland. The index is available in many libraries.

A hearing on a bill is often followed by a mark-up session, in which the bill's language is revised. A favorable vote on a marked-up bill generates a committee report, perhaps the most useful of all documents in the legislative process. The report explains the bill section by section and includes additional or dissenting views of committee members. Committee reports are printed in the *Congressional Record* or listed in Congressional Quarterly's newsletter *Congress in Print.*

After a bill is reported from a committee, it may go to the House or Senate floor for general debate. The debate is rendered in full in the *Congressional Record.* If the other chamber approves a similar but not identical bill, a conference committee of both houses is convened. When the conferees reach agreement, another document is generated—the conference report.

Assuming the conference report is approved by the full House and Senate, the measure goes to the president for his signature. It is then printed as a public law. The public law contains the legislative history, a useful summary for a writer.

Other congressional documents flow from the budget process in the House and Senate. After the president submits his proposed budget to Congress early in the year, each committee has a task to perform before the fiscal year begins October 1. Those tasks lead to more documents—from the authorizing committees (which include all House and Senate committees responsible for approving the concept of federal programs), the appropriations committees (one in the House and one in the Senate, which determine how much money each authorized program will receive), and the budget committees (one in the House and one in the Senate, which try to keep individual totals of other committees from topping a ceiling imposed by Congress on expenditures). One of the clearest explanations of the budget process and the documents flowing from it is *The Guide to the Federal Budget* by Stanley E. Collender (Washington, D.C.: Urban Institute Press).

The research and investigative arms of Congress produce numerous documents that can help writers track issues. Congressional Research Service issue briefs are listed in a monthly publication called *Update*. The briefs are unavailable to writers directly, but may be obtained through the personal staff of a member of Congress. In-depth reports from the General Accounting Office, Congressional Budget Office, and Office of Technology Assessment are available directly from those units.

Congressional caucuses produce publications regularly. Among the best are the *Weekly Bulletin* of the Environmental and Energy Study Conference and the various documents from the Democratic Study Group. "Whip advisories" from the House leadership provide a quick look at issues scheduled for debate on the chamber floor.

The administrative units of Congress publish documents that can save writers a lot of time. When Congress is meeting, the Clerk of the House issues *Calendars of the United States House of Representatives and History of Legislation*. The document is invaluable for following bills through the legislative process. The Secretary of the Senate compiles that chamber's *Calendar of Business*. Writers who want to examine expenditures of congressional committees and members' personal offices will find a wealth of detail in the quarterly *Report of the Clerk of the House* and the semi-annual *Report of the Secretary of the Senate*.

**White House Documents.** The official words of the president are recorded in *The Weekly Compilation of Presidential Documents*, published by the Office of the Federal Register and available through the Government Printing Office. It contains the president's speeches, news conferences, messages to Congress, personnel appointments, and more. Those documents are available separately to accredited journalists in the White House press room, but for writers without accreditation, the weekly booklet is handy.

The various agencies within the Executive Office of the President issue occasional documents, with the Office of Management and Budget being the most prolific. One set of documents indispensible to any writer who cares about government programs is the president's proposed budget, available near the beginning of the year. It is a four-volume set—the budget itself, a summary, an appendix, and special analyses.

**Executive Agency Documents.** Agencies spew out so many documents that a writer on just a few mailing lists may be overwhelmed. One efficient way to follow the activities of agencies is to examine the *Federal Register*, published Monday through Friday. Every agency uses the *Register* for publication of proposed rules and regulations, final rules, and legal notices. It is available through the Government Printing Office; most libraries subscribe.

Every agency is supposed to publish an agenda of regulations twice a year. The agenda provides details about current and projected rulemakings, reviews of existing regulations, and actions completed since publication of the previous agenda. Each agenda item is supposed to include the name, title, address, and telephone number of an agency employee knowledgeable about the topic. The semi-annual agendas are eventually compiled in one issue of the *Federal Register*.

The *Register* also contains notices of agency and advisory group meetings. But notices sent directly to writers from individual agencies often give more warning. For example, the *News Digest* of the Securities and Exchange Commission is timely and informative. Some agencies publish calendars listing meetings between bureaucrats and special interest group representatives.

## Books About Government

Many books, periodicals, and other documents are mentioned in the pages you just read about the public sector. This bibliography is a selective one, emphasizing vital reference works.

From the **U.S. Government Printing Office,** North Capitol and H Streets, NW, Washington, DC 20401; 202/275-2051:
*Official Congressional Directory,* issued in odd-numbered years after election of a new Congress.
*Congressional Record,* published daily when Congress is in session, published occasionally when Congress is in recess.
*How Our Laws Are Made,* a pamphlet revised from time to time.
*Federal Register,* published Monday through Friday except for federal holidays.
*The United States Government Manual,* updated annually.
*Weekly Compilation of Presidential Documents,* issued every Monday.

From **Congressional Quarterly Inc.,** 1414 22nd Street, NW, Washington, DC 20037; 202/887-8500:
*Congressional Quarterly Weekly Report,* a magazine that carries a Saturday publication date.
*Washington Information Directory,* updated annually.

An example is the public calendar published by the Food and Drug Administration.

All agencies issue reports mandated by Congress. For example, the Department of Energy publishes a multivolume program-by-program analysis because of a congressional requirement. For any writer interested in energy policy, the document is invaluable.

You may also want to consult the *Catalog of Federal Domestic Assistance,* put out by the Office of Management and Budget, which lists all domestic programs by agency, with financial information, regulations, and contact persons. Many places refer to programs by their CFDA numbers. Most libraries have this catalog; the Government Printing Office sells it.

**Court Documents.** Legal files contain a great deal of information. As already noted, Washington is the home of general

*Politics in America*, revised regularly, with each new Congress.

From **Government Research Corporation**, 1730 M Street, NW, Washington, DC 20036; 202/857-1400:
*National Journal*, a weekly magazine that carries a Saturday publication date.
*The Almanac of American Politics*, revised regularly, with each new Congress.

From **Congressional Staff Directory Ltd.**, Box 62, Mount Vernon, VA 22121; 703/765-3400:
*Congressional Staff Directory*, updated annually.
*Federal Staff Directory*, updated annually.

From **American Enterprise Institute for Public Policy Research**, 1150 17th Street, NW, Washington, DC 20036; 202/862-5800:
*Vital Statistics on Congress*, revised regularly, with each new Congress.

Some of the reference works in the bibliography are available by subscription. Some are readily available in bookstores. All the publishers mentioned are in the Washington metropolitan area. Prices change and are excluded for the sake of accuracy.

jurisdiction courts and specialized courts. Every court has a room where the public may gain access to everything on the public record. Writers who need a basic education about the federal courts should read *The Reporter and the Law* by Lyle Denniston (New York: Hastings House). Sometimes it pays just to start reading the court file, however, if a specific case is of interest. Or fishing in the court's index to cases might produce one that sounds interesting enough to examine.

## A Case Study

To research any topic, you might begin with the political science concept of "the iron triangle." That concept says policy is made through the convergence of three actors—congressional subcommittees with jurisdiction over the issue, specialists in the executive agencies with the appropriate authority, and interest groups in the private sector that would be affected by the new policy.

Actually, today the triangle has become a hexagon on many issues. The additional actors are White House staff members who sometimes override agency experts, public interest lobbyists who actively oppose narrow interests in the private sector, and the courts.

One reference book, updated annually, makes it easy for a writer to figure out where to find actors on all sides of the triangle, hexagon, or whatever. *Washington Information Directory*, published by Congressional Quarterly Inc., divides the policy spectrum into 16 chapters; each chapter has numerous subsections. The beauty of the book is that for every issue, it provides names, addresses, and telephone numbers for sources in Congress, the agencies, the White House, and the private sector.

The main problem for the knowledgeable writer is sorting through the vast amount of information available from human and documentary sources. What follows is a partial listing of resources a writer in Washington might use to learn about one sample topic—disposal of radioactive waste from nuclear power plants. Sources from the private sector are included, too. (For more detail on how to penetrate the private sector in Washington, see page 31.)

In Congress, a writer seeking information about nuclear waste disposal may go to numerous committees and subcommittees, because the topic cuts across so many jurisdictional lines. Authorizing legislation might go through these committees and subcommittees in the House: Energy and the Environment Subcommittee of the Interior and Insular Affairs Committee; Energy Conservation and Power Subcommittee of the Energy and Commerce Committee; Energy, Research and Production Subcommittee of the Science and Technology Committee; Rules Committee; Armed Services Committee (if nuclear waste from military facilities is involved); and Environment, Energy and Natural Resources Subcommittee of the Government Operations Committee.

In the Senate, authorizing legislation on nuclear waste disposal might be handled by: Energy Research and Development Subcommittee of the Energy and Natural Resources Committee;

Nuclear Regulation Subcommittee of the Environment and Public Works Committee; and Armed Services Committee.

The appropriations committees in both the House and Senate must approve sums for agency programs involving nuclear waste disposal, and the budget committees in each chamber sometimes get involved, too.

In all of the committees and subcommittees involved, there are elected members of Congress and Democratic and Republican staff knowledgeable about the topic. Transcripts of numerous committee hearings contain names of experts and their views on how to solve the gigantic problem.

The four research and investigative arms of Congress have all issued studies about nuclear waste disposal. Sample titles are "Managing Commercial High-Level Radioactive Waste" from the Office of Technology Assessment and "Is Spent Fuel or Waste from Reprocessed Spent Fuel Simpler to Dispose Of?" from the General Accounting Office.

You will also find seemingly countless sources in the executive agencies on nuclear waste disposal. The Department of Energy, Nuclear Regulatory Commission, National Aeronautics and Space Administration, United States Geological Survey, National Science Foundation, and National Bureau of Standards have all been involved. So have other agencies, as well as White House advisors. Using the *Washington Information Directory*, you can locate perhaps a dozen bureaucrats with some responsibility for nuclear waste disposal and will be given office and telephone numbers in the bargain. By consulting other sources, including agency telephone directories, you will find employees who probably work with the problem day-in, day-out. Minimal research would turn up documents such as "Nuclear Waste Isolation Activities Report" in the Energy Department's Office of Nuclear Waste Isolation; "Recommendations on National Radioactive Waste Management Policies" from the presidentially created State Planning Council on Radioactive Waste Management; and "What Are We Going to Do with Spent Fuel?" a speech by Nuclear Regulatory Commission member Victor Gilinsky.

In the private sector, there are dozens of sources in Washington. Many organizations have also issued position papers or studies. A sampling includes the Atomic Industrial

## International Resources

Washington truly is an international city. The international community thrives here and provides information for a myriad of stories. Among its highlights for writers and researchers:

**Department of State,** 2201 C Street, NW, Washington, DC 20520; 202/655-4000. Your best approach to gathering information at the State Department is through the public information office, whose staff will direct you to the appropriate area specialists and publications. Although the department's library is closed to the public, writers may use a reading room containing unclassified documents relating to international matters.

**International Development Cooperation Agency,** 320 21st Street, NW, Washington, DC 20523; 202/655-4000. This agency is comprised of three sections: Agency for International Development (AID), Overseas Private Investment Corporation, and Trade and Development Program. Again, a writer's best approach is through the public affairs office and also through the Development Information Unit, which is principally a library and is among the best sources in the city for information on developing countries. It also contains a separate collection of materials on "Women in Development."

**United States Information Agency,** 1776 Pennsylvania Avenue, NW, Washington, DC 20547; 202/655-4000. USIA works through educational and cultural exchanges, international broadcast and press activities (including Voice of America), and through films, seminars, and cultural centers to disseminate information about U.S. policies to the world. Although USIA's library, which specializes in foreign affairs, Americana, and communication, is closed to the public, journalists and researchers may be granted access. Contact the Office of Public Liaison.

**World Bank,** 1818 H Street, NW, Washington, DC 20431; 202/477-1234. The World Bank consists of three institutions: The International Bank for Reconstruction and Development (IBRD), the International Development Association (IDA), and the International Financial Corporation (IFC). The bank promotes the growth of developing economies through direct loans, assistance in evaluating development projects, and technical assistance. Especially useful for writers is the bank's bookstore, which contains a wealth of publications including staff working papers. In addition, the bank's library, operated jointly with the International Monetary Fund, provides excellent resources for journalists who are able to demonstrate a need for the materials.

**Organization of American States,** 19th Street and Constitution Avenue, NW, Washington, DC 20006; 202/789-3000. OAS maintains the Columbus Memorial Library, open to the public and useful for writers. The public information office will supply publications of the organization.

**Embassies**

The presence of the diplomatic community, represented in more than 130 embassies with many located in mansions along Massachusetts Avenue, lends glamor to Washington. The staffs of the various embassies—particularly the information officers, press counselors, and cultural and economic attaches—often provide writers with information on the countries they represent. *The Diplomatic List,* published quarterly by the State Department and available from the Government Printing Office, provides the current list of embassies and names of their professional staffs.

**International Consulting Firms**

Washington is a city of consultants, often individuals who come here to serve the government and stay on to form their own businesses. The international field includes both large and small consulting firms, most of which contract with government and private organizations in such areas as development, construction, technical analysis, and business.

Among the large firms are Bechtel; Booz-Allen & Hamilton Inc.; and Arthur D. Little Inc. In the mid-range are Robert Nathan Associates and the Planning and Development Collaborative Inc., known as PADCO. Typical of the small consulting firm is Garn Research, run by Harvey A. Garn, a former director of the Urban Economic Development Program of the Urban Institute, which specializes in economic and policy analysis.

Writers often find consultants a supplemental source of information on a range of international issues. A guide to the field is *Consultants and Consulting Organizations Directory* (Detroit: Gale Research, 1982).

—*Sandra Kirsch*

*Sandra L. Kirsch is a freelance writer and editor who specializes in international affairs. She has worked for Lambert Publications and the International Visitors Information Service, both in Washington.*

Forum, Environmental Policy Center, National Governors' Association, American Public Power Association, Critical Mass Energy Project, Union of Concerned Scientists, and Edison Electric Institute. Knowledgeable sources at local universities and consulting firms include several at Georgetown University, George Washington University, Edlow International Company, and International Energy Associates Limited.

Hundreds of magazine articles and books written by journalists and nonjournalists in Washington can provide useful guidance. A sampling of periodicals in Washington that regularly cover nuclear waste disposal would include *Inside Energy, Science, Science News, Nuclear Industry, Critical Mass Energy Journal, National Journal, Congressional Quarterly Weekly Report,* and *Chemical and Engineering News.*

## Shortcuts and Guidelines

Resident Washington correspondents who make their living covering the government for newspapers, periodicals, or broadcast media have accreditation. The credentials they receive entitle them to use media facilities in Congress, the White House, Defense Department, and State Department.

Freelance writers and other writers who fall outside the accreditation guidelines (some of which are published in the *Congressional Directory*) may gain access to congressional galleries and some other places normally closed to the general public. Showing a letter from the editor of a publication, verifying that you are working on an article, will sometimes do the trick. For details, call the Senate or the House periodical press gallery or the press offices at the White House, Defense Department, or State Department. Most other government agencies require no accreditation.

Some parts of public sector buildings are off-limits no matter who you are and what credentials you carry. That includes most of the Supreme Court building and much of the Pentagon. Writers hoping to take still or moving pictures may face special access problems. For example, there are detailed restrictions on photography in the Capitol and in congressional office buildings. Some federal agencies spell out their policies in meeting notices. Writers have tools for circumventing restrictions on their access to the public sector. The Government in the Sunshine Act and the Federal Advisory Committee Act say that designated executive agencies should meet publicly except under certain conditions. The Freedom of Information Act and the Privacy Act tell executive agencies to release information upon request unless withholding can be justified for specific reasons. Writers interested in further information can read these booklets: *An Interpretive Guide to the Government in the Sunshine Act* (compiled by the Administrative Conference of the United States and sold by the Government Printing Office) and *A Citizen's Guide on How to Use the Freedom of Information Act and the Privacy Act in Requesting Government Documents* (compiled by the House Government Operations Committee and sold by the Government Printing Office).

The Freedom of Information Act is especially useful, as far as it goes. Congress exempted itself and the courts from the law. But if a writer is trying to pry information from a Cabinet department, executive agency, or certain parts of the White House, the law can be a valuable tool.

Like all tools, it has its limits. Nine categories of information are exempted from disclosure. One category is an exemption on top of an exemption—it says if information is sealed off from disclosure under some other law, the Freedom of Information Act is superseded. There are several hundred such laws; not even the congressional subcommittees that try to track such things have identified all these back-door exemptions.

Despite the flaws in the law, it is worth a try. Requests for information can pay off handsomely. Just the act of making a request can show seriousness of purpose, leading an agency to release information without further delay. (See also page 17.)

Beyond the sources and resources enumerated in this chapter lie some general approaches that may prove helpful in writing about the federal government:

- Bureaucrats and staff, like everybody else, appreciate genuine interest in their work and respond to it. One writer says that one of her best contacts in the Congressional Office of Technology Assessment is friendly today because she dropped him a thank-you note along with a copy of the article she had written back when he was a research chief at the State Department. People really do like to see their names in print and to know that the time they gave you has a tangible result.

- You'll probably get a different reception if you are a well-known writer for a major publication than if you are unknown or write for a minor or controversial periodical. Sheer persistence may pay off with a contact in the latter case; an appeal to the public figure's desire to explain an intriguing issue may generate an interview with a lesser-known or controversial publication.
- One of the best ways to get cooperation is to know what you are talking about. Entering an interview with knowledge will earn you respect, thus breaking the ice with otherwise reluctant sources.

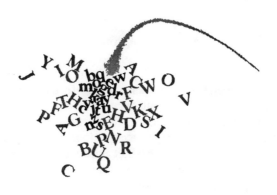

# Lobbying

## Susan J. Duncan

**W**ashington's private sector is unlike that of any other city. In large part, it exists only because the public sector—the federal government—is here. Its primary purpose is to influence legislation—in short, to lobby.

Understanding the role lobbyists play is crucial for the Washington writer who hopes to write about government, or about the business associations, trade groups, labor unions, professional societies, and public interest organizations that flourish in this city.

The migration of associations to Washington closely paralleled the growth of the government's presence in corporate boardrooms across the country. According to the American Society of Association Executives, Washington's own association for associations, trade and professional groups streamed into Washington during the 1970s at a rate of about 140 per year. That

*Susan J. Duncan is an independent writer, editor, and analyst, specializing in research, writing, and project-management services in business and government relations. Previously, she served as senior editor of* Directors & Boards, The Journal of Corporate Action.

decade also witnessed the passage of literally dozens of laws authorizing major new regulatory programs, and in many instances, new rulemaking agencies to oversee them. The Environmental Protection Agency, Occupational Safety and Health Administration, Consumer Product Safety Commission, National Highway Traffic Safety Administration, Department of Energy, Nuclear Regulatory Commission, and others were products of the seventies. Associations discovered that a Washington address was very nearly a necessity simply to monitor such federal activity, much less to influence it.

Of course, lobbying is not limited to associations. Of the 9,000 or so Washington workers attempting to steer government action in the direction of their members' or their clients' interests, associations are only the largest and most visible component, numbering about 4,000 persons at some 1,800 trade groups, professional societies, and labor unions. The 1982 edition of the annual lobbying directory, *Washington Representatives*, also identifies 1,250 representatives of more than 500 individual corporations, about the same number who advocate specific issues (such as gun control, abortion rights, or animal welfare), and about 2,500 lobbyists employed by law firms, public-relations companies, and consulting groups.

It's easy to overlook the lobbyist as a source of information. Yet, lobbyists perform research, writing, and analysis as standard services for government officials. For example, when the Food and Drug Administration decided to propose a rule under which "public" interests would receive federal funds to testify at its hearings, it published verbatim the petition written by Consumers Union. FDA announced that CU's petition was being adopted "because of its importance in evaluating the need for proposed rulemaking and in identifying the issues...." Similarly, when the Environmental Protection Agency considered such a rule for its hearings, it proposed a petition submitted by the Environmental Defense Fund. Corporate lobbyists are equally active in drafting material for legislation.

Even in Washington, where government-affairs writers presumably understand the role of private-interest groups, few seek out lobbyists as sources of information. The passage or defeat of major legislation is often described in terms of interest-group conflicts (e.g., labor vs. business, energy vs. environment), but as a quoteworthy source, the lobbyist is tainted. "Everyone knows what NRA [National Rifle Association] thinks," says one veteran correspondent who acknowledges that, in the several gun-control stories he's written, although NRA is mentioned, he has never consulted anyone there.

Other experienced Washington writers may focus exclusively on congressional and administrative sources because such officials are well known for their effusiveness, while private interests may not be so forthcoming. "The people in the legislature view publicity as the lifeblood of elective politics," notes Stephen Hess in *The Washington Reporters.*

Whatever their reasons, Washington writers who neglect the lobbyists are overlooking the very sources of information that legislators and regulators find most valuable. Far from discrediting the research supplied by private interests, government officials tend to trust it. Like a writer's, the lobbyist's reputation rides on his or her credibility. Thus, the cardinal sin of lobbying is to endanger a trusting policymaker by dissembling or by supplying incomplete or inaccurate information.

Specifically, when you call or visit for information, you can reasonably expect a lobbyist to:

- Supply background information on the industry (or movement), including its history, size characteristics (e.g., number of companies, total employees), and aggregate financial and operating statistics;
- Discuss the up-to-the-minute status of legislative or regulatory action in the area at issue; the principal players in both the public and private sectors and their apparent strategies, including coalitions; and the probable outcome, including likely compromises;
- Explain the significance and legislative or regulatory history of the issue;
- Explain the arguments behind the organization's position and rebut opposing arguments;
- Cite sources of independent support for the organization's position—scientific studies, opinion polls, etc.;
- Outline alternative approaches to resolving the issue (other than legislative or regulatory) and their feasibility and desirability from the organization's perspective;

- Point out related issues;
- Refer you to academics and other experts on the issue;
- Refer you to individual members or clients with horror stories pertaining to the issue;
- Describe the potential impact on individual members or clients, complete with detailed examples;
- Describe the potential impact on the industry as a whole—profits, inflation, unemployment, investment, international trade, etc.;
- Refer you to both opponents and allies;
- Suggest additional sources of information; and
- Supply copies of useful documents, such as testimony, white papers, and draft legislation.

Let's take a specific example of the kind of details available from lobbyists. Suppose you're writing about an Occupational Safety and Health Administration (OSHA) rule to limit worker exposure to lead by requiring that manufacturing processes be redesigned to lower the maximum concentration to 50 micrograms per cubic meter of air. Pretty dull stuff, you think. You could dutifully report the rule, its requirements, and OSHA's defense of it—all courtesy of OSHA press releases.

Or you could see what the lobbyists say about it. Since passage of the rule represents a victory for labor, let's take the business side. From the Lead Industries Association, whose members include mining companies, smelters, refiners, and manufacturers of lead products and products with lead as a component, you learn that lead is one of the most commonly used raw materials. About 120 different manufacturing industries will be required to comply with the rule, including automobiles, pottery, paint, pesticides, rubber, plastics, leather, glass, jewelry, textiles, electronic equipment, and metal smelting and refining. The largest single user of lead, however, is the battery manufacturing industry, so next you turn to the Battery Council International, a group comprised of battery manufacturers and distributors, and suppliers to the battery industry. BCI refers you to its contractor, Industrial Health Engineering Associates, who performed a cost and feasibility study of the lead standard. You also check a similar study conducted by Charles River Associates for the Lead Industries Association, and finally double check these two industry analyses against the study commissioned by OSHA from D.B. Associates.

From all these sources, you piece together the following scenario for the battery industry. Total capital costs incurred to meet the standard will range between $200-$300 million. The five largest battery companies will raise their prices by 74 cents per battery to recapture these costs, but the smaller companies, with far fewer batteries over which to spread the expense, will need to raise the price of each by about $1.48. All studies conclude that the small companies cannot raise prices by more than the 74-cent passthrough of their largest competitors or they will price themselves out of the market. Nor can they afford to absorb the additional costs. Of the 138 companies in the industry, about 100 will probably shut down, with a resulting loss of 1,000-2,000 jobs, and a sharply decreased product selection for the battery consumer. You also discover that the smaller companies could survive—*and* meet the standard—if they were permitted to require workers to wear respirators, rather than having to make expensive changes in manufacturing equipment and processes.

Your research among the lobbyists will turn up dozens of other story ideas. For instance, you may choose to write about Steelworkers Union Local 7854 in Kellogg, Idaho. Although all the major unions, including the AFL-CIO, United Autoworkers, and United Steelworkers, supported the OSHA standard, Local 7854 fought it. The 1,500 members agreed that respirators and other controls were preferable to losing their jobs at Bunker Hill Company's lead smelter. Owners of the smelter cannot afford to meet the lead standard and will be forced either to sell the smelter or to close it. No one is interested in buying a plant in need of millions of dollars worth of new equipment. The governor of Idaho warns that if the smelter, the state's second largest employer, shuts down, repercussions could eliminate $200 million each year from the Idaho economy. The area surrounding Kellogg already has a 20 percent unemployment rate.

Once you're convinced that lobbyists supply some of the best story leads, your first step will be to identify which lobbyists are involved in your topic.

Consult the trade press or technical journals in your field for those associations active in lobbying. If your specific issue (or a similar one) has come before Congress or an agency in the past

## Who Watches the Watchdogs?

For more than a decade, a strong corps of public interest organizations has set up camp in Washington, keeping tabs on virtually every government agency and private industry. These are the groups that make sure that the government "watchdog" agencies are doing their jobs.

Besides offering an alternative to many business and government stories, most of the groups listed below can provide a wealth of information about the industries and agencies they cover. In fact, many of these groups specialize in disseminating information that they believe has been kept from the public.

Since most of these groups have small staffs and even smaller budgets, you may be forced to do most of the legwork yourself; these groups will provide you with the contacts and, often, with access to their extensive files and libraries.

Here is a sampling of the major public interest groups:

**American Association of Retired Persons,** 1919 K Street, NW, Washington, DC 20006; 202/872-4700. Seeks to improve every aspect of living for older people, including Social Security reform, prescription drug prices, and senior citizen housing.

**Center for Auto Safety,** 1223 Dupont Circle Building, Washington, DC 20036; 202/659-1226. Formerly part of the Nader network, this group performs research and participates in litigation in the area of auto safety.

**Center for Law and Social Policy,** 1751 N Street, NW, Washington, DC 20036; 202/872-0670. A public interest law firm that represents citizens before regulatory agencies and the courts.

**Common Cause,** 2030 M Street, NW, Washington, DC 20036; 202/833-1200. This is a lobbying organization concerned with government reform. Key issues include election funding and lobby disclosure.

**Consumer Affairs Committee/Americans for Democratic Action,** 3005 Audubon Terrace, NW, Washington, DC 20008; 202/244-4080. Primarily a research group, they focus on supermarket prices and product safety.

**Consumer Federation of America,** 1314 14th Street, NW, Washington, DC 20005; 202/387-6121. This is a federation of more than

200 local consumer groups focusing on the entire spectrum of consumer issues.

**Defenders of Wildlife,** 1244 19th Street, NW, Washington, DC 20036; 202/659-9510. Works to defend wildlife through public education, legislative action, and court suits.

**Environmental Action Foundation,** 731 Dupont Circle Building, Washington, DC 20036; 202/833-1845. An education and research organization that publishes information on a wide range of environmental issues, as well as utility rate structure, nuclear power, and water management.

**Environmental Defense Fund,** 1525 18th Street, NW, Washington, DC 20036; 202/833-1484. A national organization of scientists, lawyers, and economists working to protect the public interest in the areas of environmental quality, energy, and health.

**National Consumers League,** 1522 K Street, NW, Washington, DC 20005; 202/797-7600. The oldest national consumer group, it conducts consumer information programs in the areas of product safety, food and nutrition, credit, insurance, and health care.

**National Insurance Consumer Organization,** 344 Commerce Street, Alexandria, VA 22314; 703/549-8050. Covers insurance reform and promotes public understanding of the insurance industry.

**Public Citizen,** 2000 P Street, NW, Washington, DC 20036; 202/293-9142. This is the umbrella organization for the Ralph Nader-affiliated groups, including: **Center for the Study of Responsive Law** (1530 P Street, NW, Washington, DC 20005; 202/387-8030), which conducts a wide variety of research and educational projects; **Critical Mass Energy Project** (215 Pennsylvania Avenue, SE, Washington, DC 20003; 202/546-4790), focusing on nuclear and other energy issues; **Congress Watch** (215 Pennsylvania Avenue, SE, Washington, DC 20003; 202/546-4996), the advocacy arm of the Nader network, which lobbies Congress on a variety of issues; **Health Research Group** (2000 P Street, NW, Washington, DC 20036; 202/872-0320), working on consumer health issues, including dangerous drugs and medical devices; and **Tax Reform Research Group** (215 Pennsylvania Avenue, SE, Washington, DC 20003; 202/544-1710), focusing on national and local tax reform issues.

**Telecommunications Research Action Center,** 1530 P Street, NW, Washington, DC 20005; 202/462-2520. Focuses on broadcasting, telephone, and other telecommunications issues.

*—Joel Makower*

(and very few are completely original), check the agency docket for the names of those who filed comments and the hearing transcripts for those who testified before congressional committees. Chances are good these same groups will either be lobbying on your issue or will refer you to someone who is. When you interview government officials or congressional staff, ask for the names of major lobbyists. ("Can you recommend two or three people in industry I could talk to about this?") Some sources will freely volunteer this information.

Under the 1946 Federal Regulation of Lobbying Act, certain lobbyists must register with the Secretary of the Senate and the Clerk of the House; they must identify for whom they lobby, on what issues, and, in some instances, how much they spend each quarter. These registrations appear regularly in both the *Congressional Record* and the *Congressional Quarterly Weekly Report*. However, only congressional lobbyists are subject to registration (those who lobby executive or independent agencies are excluded), and even among these, numerous loopholes limit the number affected. For example, certain types of lobbying, such as grass-roots campaigns and committee testimony, were exempted from the law. Moreover, no one verifies registrations or investigates failure to register.

Nevertheless, this is the most specific data source at present. For instance, a typical entry reveals that Washington lobbyist Eugene Stewart lobbied in the second quarter of 1982 to "amend tariff schedules of the U.S. to align rates on fresh-cut roses with those imposed by the European Economic Community," on behalf of Roses Inc. of Haslett, Michigan.

You may also turn to annual directories of interest groups, although most of these reveal only the general subject areas of the groups' operations, not their lobbying activities in specific issues. Four directories are available in many public libraries:

- *Encyclopedia of Associations*, published by Gale Research Company, and indexed by subject, key word, geographic region, proper name, and names of key executives;
- *National Trade and Professional Associations of the United States and Canada and Labor Unions*, published by Columbia Books, and indexed by key word, geographic region, budget, proper name, and name of executive director;

- *Washington Representatives*, published by Columbia Books, a true lobbying directory, indexed by name of lobbyist, name of client, country, and subject; and
- *Washington Information Directory*, published by Congressional Quarterly, and indexed by subject and proper name. This directory is divided into chapters, each on a particular topic (e.g., Congress & Politics, Economics & Business, Law & Justice), listing both public- and private-sector organizations and a reference bibliography.

And, for the price of a phone call, Information Central, a service of the American Society of Association Executives, will refer you to an association in the subject or industry of your choice. Dial 202/626-2742.

When you're confronted with a number of groups lobbying on the same issue (food safety, for instance), you can make an initial determination of which groups exercise the greatest potential influence by evaluating membership characteristics. In their book, *Interest Group Politics in America*, political scientists Ronald Hrebenar and Ruth Scott enumerate these elements of lobbying power: (1) number of members, (2) geographic distribution of the membership, (3) group demographics—income, education, occupation, (4) presence of prestige or celebrity members, (5) member commitment, (6) group cohesion, (7) market share (the ratio of members to potential members), (8) quality of the group's leadership and staff, and (9) financial resources of the group.

Suppose you'd like to contact several unions in different industries, all of which are lobbying on your issue, or, as in the lead example above, you're looking for lobbyists in a variety of industries, all of which are manufacturers. Your best bet is first to locate a horizontal organization that can then recommend the vertical groups most active in your issue.

A horizontal or "umbrella" organization cuts across many different industries, while a vertical or industry-specific group is restricted to one trade. For example, the Asphalt Emulsion Manufacturers Association, the Envelope Manufacturers Association, and the Southern Furniture Manufacturers Association are all vertical organizations. But both the individual members of each group—asphalt emulsion manufacturers, envelope manufacturers, and southern furniture manufacturers—and the groups

## Covering the Umbrella Organizations

| Name | Membership | Address |
|------|-----------|---------|
| American Society of Association Executives | 8,000 executives of nonprofit membership organizations | 1575 I Street, NW; 202/626-2742 |
| National Association of Manufacturers | 12,000 manufacturers; 250 local, state, and national manufacturing associations | 1776 F Street, NW; 202/626-3700 |
| National Association of Wholesaler-Distributors | 43,000 wholesaler-distributors and local, state, and national wholesaler-distributors associations | 1725 K Street, NW; 202/626-0885 |
| International Franchise Association | 400 companies that use the franchise method of distribution | 1025 Connecticut Avenue, NW; 202/659-0790 |

themselves may belong to the umbrella organization, the National Association of Manufacturers.

Similarly, the American Retail Federation represents national and state associations of retailers, as well as major retail corporations; the National Association of Wholesaler-Distributors represents national wholesale distribution associations (e.g., the National Fastener Distributors Association, the National Beer Wholesalers Association, the National Independent Bank Equipment Suppliers Association); and the International Franchise Association represents franchising companies in all industries worldwide. Other business groups are still broader-based, welcoming all sectors—manufacturing, retailing, wholesaling, etc. These are discussed below, followed by brief descriptions of the primary labor and consumer umbrella organizations.

| American Retail Federation | major retailers; 80 state and national retail associations | 1616 H Street, NW; 202/783-7971 |
| --- | --- | --- |
| U.S. Chamber of Commerce | 250,000 individuals and companies; 4,000 trade associations; and state, local, and regional chambers | 1615 H Street, NW; 202/659-6000 |
| Business Roundtable | chief executive officers of largest 200 corporations | 1828 L Street, NW; 202/659-6000 |
| National Federation of Independent Business | 500,000 professionals and small-business owners | 600 Maryland Avenue, SW; 202/554-9000 |
| AFL-CIO | 15 million union members; 900 local, state, and national unions | 815 16th Street, NW; 202/637-5000 |

**Business.** The U.S. Chamber of Commerce, founded in 1912, is a federation of some 250,000 individuals and companies, 4,000 trade and professional groups, and state, local, and regional chambers of commerce. Although the Chamber likes to point out that about 85 percent of its individual business members employ fewer than 100 workers, it has traditionally pressed for big-business interests. Policy is formulated through 20 executive committees, and the Chamber takes positions on roughly 60 issues each year.

A Chamber brochure lists the names and telephone numbers of "staff specialists" in more than 50 different legislative and regulatory areas. Chamber publications include a weekly newspaper, *Washington Report*; a weekly legislative and a monthly regulatory newsletter; and a monthly magazine, *Nation's Busi-*

*ness.* Books, studies, and reports issued by organizational units (such as business-government affairs, human and community resources, resources and environmental quality, and economic policy) are described in the booklet, *Information Resources.*

In recent years, the Chamber has mounted a mammoth grass-roots communications program, including the production of weekly TV and radio programs and operation of its own TV network, Biznet, which beams five hours of business and government news each day to its subscribers. (Grass-roots mobilization is the Chamber's lobbying forte.)

The Business Roundtable, although its headquarters are in New York, accomplishes much of its work through its Washington office. Membership in the Roundtable is restricted to the chief executive officers (CEOs) of the nation's 200 largest corporations. Unlike the other lobbying groups discussed here, the Roundtable is strictly do-it-yourself. There are no paid, professional lobbyists; instead, CEOs of such corporate giants as General Motors, General Electric, IBM, AT&T, U.S. Steel, Standard Oil, and Citibank put in personal appearances on the Hill. This tactic succeeds because the sheer stature of the members ensures access. Notes one congressional staff member: "Washington reps will see a legislative assistant. But the chairman of Du Pont, say, will get to see the Senator." *Congressional Quarterly* quotes an aide: "There would be very few members of Congress who would *not* meet with the president of a Business Roundtable corporation, even if there were no district connection." Because of CEO time constraints, however, the Roundtable focuses on only a few important issues each year.

In contrast to other groups, the Roundtable shuns publicity and aims for a low profile. Since its creation in 1972, it has proven the lobbying effectiveness of direct contact alone, without the need for supplemental grass-roots mailings, ad campaigns, press conferences, and the like. Its 15 task forces conduct extensive research among the member companies when necessary to support the Roundtable's positions.

The National Federation of Independent Business (NFIB) is the principal umbrella organization for small business. Formed in 1943, its 500,000 members, small-business owners and professional people, determine the organization's legislative positions by vote on four to five issues eight times each year. With headquarters in San Mateo, California, NFIB's Washington office is responsible for legislative, research, and public affairs. NFIB increased its visibility and improved its track record when it hired a former congressman as its chief lobbyist in 1973. The Federation compiles quarterly statistical surveys of small-business conditions.

**Labor.** The AFL-CIO, with headquarters in Washington, is by far the largest lobby. Its 15 million members belong to more than 100 separate affiliated unions (e.g., plumbers, garment workers, meat cutters, public employees). Policy is established by an executive council composed of the AFL-CIO president and the presidents of about one-third of the affiliates. Because of its diverse membership, virtually no issue fails to interest one or more of the affiliated unions. Dozens of issues attract the attention of the entire AFL-CIO each year.

**Consumer.** Numerous groups do battle for the consumer. Among these is Public Citizen, the Ralph Nader conglomerate of consumer groups, founded in 1973 "to provide effective citizen advocacy in the most pressing problems at the least cost by using the services of volunteers, keeping expenses as low as possible, and hiring dedicated professionals who are willing to work long hours for modest salaries." It is not a membership organization, but about 200,000 supporters make yearly contributions.

The Nader affiliates include the Public Citizen Litigation Group, the Tax Reform Research Group, the Public Citizen Health Research Group (investigates health care, workplace safety, drug regulation, food additives, medical devices, environmental influences), the Critical Mass Energy Project (opposed to nuclear power; promotes conservation and renewable energy sources), and Congress Watch (lobbies on energy, taxes, food and product safety, and other consumer issues). Public Citizen publishes four periodicals: *The Public Citizen, People and Taxes, Critical Mass Journal,* and *Congress Watcher.*

Nader places heavy emphasis on two conventional lobbying techniques: publicity and direct contact. He also advocates litigation as a lobbying tool. Rather than conduct grass-roots campaigns, Nader encourages the formation of state and local

## Books on Lobbying

American Society of Association Executives. *Setting Up a Government Relations Campaign.* Washington, D.C.: ASAE, 1982.

deKieffer, Donald. *How to Lobby Congress, A Guide for the Citizen Lobbyist.* New York: Dodd, Mead & Company, 1981.

Fox, Harrison, Jr., and Martin Schnitzer. *Doing Business in Washington: How to Win Friends and Influence Government.* New York: The Free Press, 1981.

Hess, Stephen. *The Washington Reporters.* Washington, D.C.: The Brookings Institution, 1981.

Hrebenar, Ronald and Ruth Scott. *Interest Group Politics in America.* Englewood Cliffs, New Jersey: Prentice-Hall Inc., 1982.

Ornstein, Norman and Shirley Elder. *Interest Groups, Lobbying and Policymaking.* Washington, D.C.: Congressional Quarterly Press, 1978.

Peters, Charles. *How Washington Really Works.* Reading, Massachusetts: Addison-Wesley Publishing Company, 1980.

*The Washington Lobby.* Third Edition. Washington, D.C.: Congressional Quarterly Inc., 1979.

Weinberg, Steve. *Trade Secrets of Washington Journalists.* Washington, D.C.: Acropolis Books Ltd., 1981.

"Public Interest Research Groups." But since none of the PIRGs are accountable either to Nader or to Public Citizen, some in Congress believe this approach is ineffective and that lack of district clout is a serious hindrance to consumer lobbying. Nevertheless, committees continue to turn to Nader to request research and testimony refuting the corporate position on any given issue. As a result, the Nader conglomerate churns out a staggering number of studies and reports for a group of its size.

**Think Tanks.** Strictly speaking, think tanks cannot be classified as lobbying organizations. Funded by foundations and corporations and established to research, analyze, and recommend action on public-policy issues, they stop short of taking their cases directly to Congress, unless invited to present their findings. Instead, they rely on indirect routes, using the media (both print and broadcast) as intermediaries. This tactic works well because the think tanks command much respect among the media. Typically, their resident scholars are either drawn from high-level government posts or will succeed to them. In addition, the think tanks stand at the ready as authoritative information resources for the press. Whenever you require scholarly research in support of (or opposition to) a particular position on a controversial issue, you can generally get it from a think tank. Despite their claims to be free of any political orientation, all can easily be tagged liberal or conservative, Democratic or Republican. Like most lobbying groups, think tanks also sponsor press conferences and seminars, but here research, not politics, is publicized. A review of think-tank publications will frequently turn up little-noted problems, questions, and effects associated with government policies or programs.

Among the most influential Washington think tanks are the two granddaddies, The Brookings Institution and the American Enterprise Institute for Public Policy Research (AEI).

"Knowledge will forever govern ignorance and a people who mean to be their own governors must arm themselves with the power knowledge gives" is the Brookings Institution motto. Founded in 1927, it is the more academically oriented of the two. In its efforts to produce "standard reference works," policymakers sometimes accuse Brookings of being too slow to be useful. Consequently, the institution is attempting to cut the long lag between research and publication, and has initiated a number of devices, including congressional seminars and circulation of staff working papers, to improve its timeliness. Nevertheless, "Brookings has neither the capacity nor the desire to have its staff members issue 'position papers' on . . . every important question that policymakers face," says President Bruce MacLaury.

Its research focuses on three areas: economics, government, and foreign policy. Although primarily a book publisher, Brookings has launched a new quarterly magazine, *The Brookings Review*, to highlight continuing research, partly in response to the "increased competition for influence" in the think-tank community. Also of interest is the Brookings *Directory of Scholars*.

AEI has a motto, too: "Competition of ideas is fundamental to a free society. A free society, if it is to remain free, cannot permit itself to be dominated by one strain of thought." Founded in 1943, AEI contributed a number of its resident scholars to the Reagan Administration, including Arthur Burns, Jeane Kirkpatrick, James C. Miller III, and Murray Weidenbaum. AEI maintains a high profile through a legislative analysis service provided free of charge to members of Congress. About 90 percent of Congress has requested one or more of these analyses, each of which summarizes a bill's history and provisions, and offers "a balanced statement of the arguments, pro and con, together with supporting authorities" (but no recommendation). The analyses are also available to the public for purchase.

In addition to books and studies in 11 different program areas (e.g., energy, health, economics, national defense), AEI also publishes three magazines, *Public Opinion, Regulation,* and *Foreign Policy and Defense Review,* and a newsletter, *The AEI Economist.*

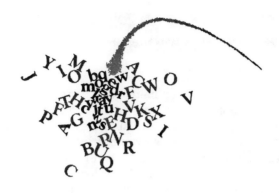

# Libraries and Archives

## Jutta Hennig

A well-traveled Washington writer, Luree Miller, whose non-fiction books and magazine articles have required exploring and checking innumerable sources in many countries, comments on Washington libraries:

> After having worked in other countries where libraries are under lock and key and library users must be screened and have sponsors, it is a thrill to come to Washington. Nowhere else in the world is so much information so available to the public or librarians so well trained to serve the people rather than simply to protect collections. We often take this for granted, but the American attitude about the public's right to know is unique.

One-sixth of all the library resources in the United States are

---

*Jutta Hennig works in Washington as a bilingual journalist and researcher on assignment for American and German publications. She uses area libraries and archives to research topics ranging from U.S. production and storage of chemical weapons to international banking practices.*

housed in the Washington metropolitan area, giving writers an unparalleled opportunity to exercise the right to know. The Library of Congress, the many libraries maintained by government agencies and private organizations, and the university libraries, plus archives of records and papers, are all available. With so much information on file, writers need only learn which drawer to pull, which book to summon, which catalog to consult. The more informed their choice of a library, the easier it will be to find the needed information.

## Library of Congress

*Thomas Jefferson Building, 1st Street and Independence Avenue, SE, Washington, DC 20540;*
*John Adams Building, 2nd Street and Independence Avenue, SE, Washington, DC 20540;*
*James Madison Memorial Building, 101 Independence Avenue, SE, Washington, DC 20540*

The Library of Congress (LC) is the largest library in the world, housing approximately 81.5 million items and accumulating new ones at a rate of about 1.5 million pieces a year. If you looked at every item in the collections at a rate of one a minute and worked at this task eight hours a day, five days a week, it would take 640 years to see everything.

Given this staggering fact, how do you begin to approach the Library of Congress? It is important to keep in mind that you must do your reading and note-taking on the premises as LC books are not available for borrowing. Therefore it is vital to know exactly which collections you need to consult and to find out first if they can be obtained from a lending library should you prefer to work somewhere else. LC librarians strongly recommend that you exhaust other sources before you request the heavily used LC material. They refer to the LC as a "library of last resort." But it is inspiring to sit with other researchers and scholars under the magnificent Great Dome of the Main Reading Room. You can contemplate its soaring vault while waiting for your books to arrive from the stacks. During peak usage periods that wait may take as long as an hour and a half, so it helps to bring other material to work on until you have your books. Still, while it is true that you may get many materials faster from other libraries, most writers will find that they will quite often want and need to visit the LC. Therefore, it's important to learn your way around.

**Guides.** To make an informed decision about whether or not to use the LC for a given project, you should read the free guides the library offers at the Research Guidance Office in the Main Reading Room. In addition, you may want to familiarize yourself with the library by reading *Guide to the Library of Congress* (1982), available for purchase at the library giftshop. The Research Guidance Office is a necessary stop even for seasoned library users, because the staff will map out a research strategy for you. "If you do not ask for help, you are likely to miss a lot of material without ever realizing it," one librarian says.

While in the Research Guidance Office, pick up the free booklet *Information for Readers in the Library of Congress*. It explains how to reserve up to three books for three days and how to get a study shelf, which not only gives you space but also the right to reserve books for an extended period of time. If you are engaged in fulltime research using the collections of the library, you may apply for a study facility on a short- or long-term basis. Given the waiting lists for study facilities, it may help your case to send a letter from your publisher about your upcoming book with your application. If that does not apply, you may want to include some clips and a resume. Barring that, appeal to your congressional representative for help.

If you prefer not to wait for your material at a desk in a reading room, you may consider putting in a "Hold" or an "Overnight Call." In the Main Reading Room of the Thomas Jefferson Building, a book on "Hold" will be held under your name at the Central Desk until the end of the day; for "Overnight Call," the book will be delivered at the beginning of the next day. Some writers have the foresight to call the Central Desk to ask if their books ordered on "Overnight Call" have arrived before making a special trip. If the librarians are not too busy, they may be willing to check, although it is not part of their job.

**Catalogs and Data Bases.** To get a good grasp on the library's holdings, use the catalogs and aids in the special reading rooms as well as the main card catalog and the computer catalog in the Thomas Jefferson Building. The computer catalog in the Main Reading Room complements the card catalog, which lists only books acquired and cataloged before 1980. The computer catalog gives users access to several in-house LC data bases. One data base within that system covers English language books on all subjects since 1968, French language books since 1973, and Spanish, German, and Portuguese language books since 1975.

Other strong points of the in-house computer system are the five legislative information files containing information about bills and resolutions. The files cover the 93rd to the 97th Congresses; they let you find quick answers to such questions as "How many bills on X subject did Senator Y introduce or co-sponsor in the 97th Congress?"

Another data base contains references to selected periodical articles since 1976, Government Printing Office publications, United Nations documents, and publications by lobbying groups. Periodicals in the file do not cover literary, scientific, or technical subjects, and deal with issues from a policy point of view only.

Although on-line searches at the LC are free, it may be more useful to go to area libraries that use on-line search services produced by commercial vendors. These may include more than one hundred data bases, covering periodical articles on a much wider range of subjects. All area libraries charge a fee for such searches. For a listing of available on-line services, consult the *On-line Directory: Search Services Available in Metropolitan Washington*, published by the Metropolitan Washington Council of Governments.

**National Referral Center.** This is a free referral service through which the library makes available the names of organizations willing to provide information on given subjects. The computerized file with a subject index covers 13,000 organizations in a range of fields, including arts and humanities. The Center maintains systematic coverage only for resources in the United States, but the file includes some international and foreign resources.

**Telephone Reference.** General reference is provided through the library's telephone reference service during regular library hours. Reference librarians on duty will help with questions that may be answered from easily accessible reference tools and through the in-house computer search services. If an answer cannot be found within a few minutes, librarians may offer to call you back or may refer you to other sources that allow you to pursue the research on your own.

When using telephone reference, be sure you have a specific question. Callers with global requests ("What do you have on oil companies?") may be asked to identify a more specific question through research at their neighborhood libraries.

**Technical Reports.** With more than three million reports available for public use at the Science Reading Room, the library has one of the world's largest technical reports collections. Technical reports are generated by contractors and by government agencies, such as the Department of Defense or the Department of Energy, in response to a government contract. They may be final or interim reports and should not be confused with market survey reports produced by private consulting firms.

Technical reports are a major vehicle for reporting new trends in science and technology, including the social sciences and education. "With technical reports you can get access to the most current edge of scientific advance," says Carl Green, head of the Technical Reports Section. "These reports often appear six months before a journal article and sometimes two years before a monograph."

**Dissertations and Microfilm.** For recent information on any given subject, you may want to consider the vast collection of dissertations, most of which are stored on microfilm in the Microfilm Reading Room of the Thomas Jefferson Building. Access is gained through an index stored in this room, although a few dissertations appear in the main catalog of the main reading room.

The Microfilm Reading Room may provide you with several other relevant sources. There is the Foreign Broadcast Information Service, which summarizes daily the coverage of an issue in the foreign press and broadcast media. English translations of complete foreign language articles on a range of subjects are available in the Joint Publications Research Service.

**Congressional Research Service.** The Congressional Research Service (CRS), which works exclusively for Congress, prepares reports, studies, and issue briefs on a range of topical subjects. Some of that material is in the public domain and may be obtained from several sources. Before buying the material from the Government Printing Office, you may want to try your senator or representative's office. Sometimes issue briefs, which provide background information for members of Congress, may be obtained upon request from the library's information office in the Madison Building.

**CIA Reports.** Reports released to the public by the Central Intelligence Agency are for sale at the Photoduplication Service of the Library of Congress. The reports, which are sometimes called CIA Reference Aids, deal with such topics as economic and political structures in foreign countries. A listing of released reports is available there for reference only, but may also be purchased.

Any writer serious about the craft will want to visit the LC, take a tour (offered each day), and learn to use the various collections. And even those writers whose work requires little research may want to enjoy the experience of simply sitting in the octagonal Main Reading Room and enjoying its atmosphere.

## The National Archives and Records Service

*Pennsylvania Avenue at 8th Street, NW, Washington, DC 20408*

The National Archives and Records Service (NARS), best-known as the resting place of the originals of the Declaration of Independence, the Constitution, and the Bill of Rights, also contains the Watergate tapes of Richard Nixon. This range from the sublime to the ridiculous may suggest why writers use the Archives for more than the popular genealogical research inspired by Alex Haley's *Roots*. Though it's true that anyone writing about family origins will want to check the Archives' pension and census records (as well as the LC Local History and Genealogy Room), materials stored in the Archives include maps, microfilm, motion pictures, aerial and still photographs, and sound recordings. Most of the materials were originally created and received by government bodies in transaction of their official business or in pursuance of law (the Nixon tapes being an exception to the latter).

Besides the main NARS building on Pennsylvania Avenue, there is an annex on 8th Street; the Stock Film Library in Arlington, Virginia, near the Pentagon; and the Washington National Records Center in Suitland, Maryland, which can be reached from the District by a shuttle bus from the main building.

There are approximately 460 record groups in the system administered by NARS. The National Archives in Washington is one of the 15 federal records centers; 11 of these are open for research. NARS also administers seven fully operating Presidential libraries, and two Presidential Papers projects.

A number of publications provide explanations of the collection, services, research rooms, and other facilities of the Archives. *A Researcher's Guide to the National Archives* is a free pamphlet explaining such matters as the identification card you need to work in the Archives. Writers new to the area will also want to catch an interesting tour conducted daily from the lobby of the main building.

The most detailed in-depth guide is published by NARS as the *Guide to the National Archives of the United States* (1974), which is for sale by the Government Printing Office. If you do not want to spend the money, get one of the free general guides and/or guides to specific record groups and subject matters the NARS publishes. There is a limited supply available for single copy distribution to scholars and institutions by writing to the Publications Sales Branch, General Services Administration, Washington, DC 20408. Among the general publications, *A Select List of Publications of the National Archives and Records Service* (General Information Leaflet, Number 3), and a guide for use of records, *Regulations for the Public Use of Records in the National Archives and Records Service* (General Information Leaflet, Number 2). The free pamphlets are available from the Publications Office (Room G-6) at the ground floor of the main building.

Consultants employed at the Archives are helpful. Few people using the facility have a concept of how its records are organized or how to use the reference aids, which differ from those used for library holdings. Materials are not arranged by subject matter, but by agency of origin in record groups. A

---

## Recommended Reading

Check the following references at your library:
*American Library Directory*, 34th edition, 1981.
*Directory of Archives and Manuscript Repositories in the United States*, 1978.
*Directory of Special Libraries and Information Centers*, 7th edition, 1982.
*Guide to the National Archives of the United States*, 1974.
*Guide to Genealogical Research in the National Archives*, scheduled for spring 1983.
*Library and Reference Facilities in the Area of the District of Columbia*, 11th edition, 1983.
*MAGS: Metropolitan Area Guide to Serials*, 1983 edition.
*Special Collections in the Library of Congress*, 1980.
*Subject Directory of Special Libraries and Information Centers*, 1981.
*Union List of Legal Periodicals*, 4th edition, 1982.

---

record group often consists of the combined records of a particular government agency or department.

Overall, the organization of the National Archives and of most other archives is guided by the principle of provenance. That is, archives try to keep the records of a given agency in the same arrangement in which they were organized originally by the agency that created them.

To gain access to the records, you may use various aids including guides that briefly describe all or part of an archive's holdings; inventories that list part or all of the materials in a record group; or calendars in which individual documents are chronologically arranged. Occasionally, there may be indexes to parts of a record group.

Entities creating the records now stored at the National Archives include Congress, the White House, federal courts, executive departments, and agencies. Collectively, the records preserved cover the history of the American government from its establishment through the mid-twentieth century. Although only valuable records are being stored, there are more than 1.5 million cubic feet of materials in the National Archives here.

A very small part of these holdings are gift collections consisting of donated materials and historical manuscripts related to activities of the U.S. government. For instance, the gift collection on Materials Relating to Polar Regions contains papers and materials of American explorers.

Presidential and personal papers of political figures such as Henry Morgenthau are in the custody of the various presidential libraries throughout the country. Within the National Archives complex in Washington there is also a library, which has more than 180,000 books and pamphlets on U.S. history, specifically the administrative history of federal agencies.

Most records in the Archives are easily accessible, but some are restricted because of their confidential character. Consultants will give details on restrictions and handling instructions.

The Archives holds a small collection of records seized by U.S. authorities from foreign governments during World War II, most notably from Germany (Record Group 242). These records have not been assimilated into the collection of World War II Crime Records (Record Group 238), which include materials used in the Nuremburg Tribunal and subsequent war crime trials.

For writers engaged in historical research, becoming familiar with the National Archives remains a must.

## Smithsonian Institution Libraries

As a trust establishment of the United States, the Smithsonian Institution is a vast storehouse of treasures and bric-a-brac. However, it is also a research institution of great distinction, and as such it maintains a system of libraries, comprised of 36 geographically dispersed branches and satellites, organized with centralized administration, collections, and systems planning. Local Smithsonian libraries are: Central Reference and Loan Services, Special Collections, Museum Reference Center, Chesapeake Bay Center for Environmental Studies, National Air and Space Museum, National Museum of African Art, National Museum of American History, National Zoological Park, and Radiation Biology Laboratory. The libraries collect materials pertinent to the work of the Smithsonian, with strengths in natural science, art, history, and technology. The collections number about one million volumes.

The libraries serve primarily the scholars and researchers working and visiting at the Smithsonian Institution. However, the public may borrow materials through the interlibrary loan system available to them in public, special, college, and university libraries. On-site use of materials may be arranged by telephoning the appropriate branch for an appointment or by contacting Central Reference and Loan Services (National Museum of Natural History, Room 25, Washington, DC 20560; 202/357-2139). A series of free guides on the branches and their services is also available from Central Reference and Loan Services.

Independent Smithsonian libraries not part of this system are the libraries located in the National Museum of American Art/National Portrait Gallery, the Freer Gallery, the Hirshhorn Museum, and the Woodrow Wilson International Center for Scholars.

**National Anthropological Archives.** Materials in the National Anthropological Archives include papers of individual anthropologists and records of anthropological and Indian organizations. In addition to such records, the holdings on North American Indians consist of linguistic, ethnological, archeological, and physical anthropological materials, including 300,000 photographs. A flyer published by the Archives provides an overview. More detailed information about much of the older material is in the four volumes of *Manuscripts at the National Anthropological Archives* (1975).

**Archives of American Art.** Manuscript, photographic, and printed materials on the development of visual arts in America since the 18th century are maintained at the Archives of American Art in the National Museum of American Art/National Portrait Gallery Building. The collections are comprised of millions of items, including personal papers of artists as well as records of businesses and organizations involved with art.

**Smithsonian Institution Archives.** The Smithsonian Institution Archives serves as the repository for the official records of the Institution and the personal papers of administrative and scientific staff and related professional organizations. The collection of more than 8,000 cubic feet of archival material is particularly strong in the history of natural science. The *Guide to the Smithsonian Archives* provides details.

## Special Libraries

There are numerous special libraries in Washington. They are maintained by trade and professional associations, hospitals, think tanks, embassies, unions, law firms, museums, federal and state agencies, international organizations, and a host of other groups.

Special libraries offer more depth on fewer subjects than public or university libraries and are equipped to provide immediate, practical information for their clientele. The subject areas covered by the holdings are closely related to the field in which the parent organization works and are further characterized by an organization's objectives, finances, size, and age. It is easy to get a general idea of the subjects represented, for instance, in the library of the AFL-CIO or the Canadian embassy. However, to learn about specific holdings, you need to study directories such as *Library and Reference Facilities in the Area of the District of Columbia*, which are available in the LC and in public libraries. Also helpful is a series of Scholars' Guides published by the Smithsonian's Woodrow Wilson International Center for Scholars. Each guide lists libraries and archives with holdings relevant to a specific subject.

Before you marvel at all this information at your fingertips, you should be aware that special libraries are not open to everyone. Primarily they are meant to support the staff or members of the organization. Restrictions on use vary from library to library, as does access to on-line bibliographic data bases. In general, special libraries maintained by private organizations tend to be more restrictive than those maintained by the government with tax dollars. The majority of government libraries are open to the public, but some are closed because of the nature of the department's or agency's work. Most federal libraries do not provide on-line data-base searches for outside users.

Many private institutions give permission to qualified outside researchers by appointment only. Some organizations may even be reluctant to say they have a library or information center

## Dialing for Data

**Library of Congress**
General Information . . . . . . . . . . . . . . . . . . . . . . . 202/287-5000
Press Information . . . . . . . . . . . . . . . . . . . . . . . 202/287-5108
Forms Request . . . . . . . . . . . . . . . . . . . . . . . . 202/287-9100
Central Desk . . . . . . . . . . . . . . . . . . . . . . . . . 202/287-7467
National Referral Center . . . . . . . . . . . . . . . . . . 202/287-5670
Telephone Reference . . . . . . . . . . . . . . . . . . . . 202/287-5522

**National Archives and Records Service**
General Information . . . . . . . . . . . . . . . . . . . . . 202/523-3218
Archives Press Information . . . . . . . . . . . . . . . . 202/523-3099

**Martin Luther King Memorial Library**
Reference and Information . . . . . . . . . . . . . . . . 202/727-1126

when you call to inquire. Others maintain only small resource centers here. This is the case with the American Film Institute (AFI) at the Kennedy Center, which offers a small reference collection and help in locating other facilities for your research.

There is some debate about how to gain access to information from the 2,600 nonprofit associations in the area. It is true that you do not have to be a member of an association to request information. It is also true that a nonprofit association may be in violation of antitrust laws if it refuses to give nonmembers information it makes available to members, as some guides to Washington information sources have pointed out. However, association lawyers say this is not a particularly fruitful argument to use when trying to gain access to an association library, because it is modified by so many contingencies.

Before you suspect a conspiracy of librarians, consider that restricting access for outside users is a necessity for many special libraries, which have limited space, a small collection, and a small staff. Most will try to accommodate people with a legitimate research need that cannot be filled elsewhere. Occasionally, a bona fide press pass carrying your picture and name will quickly get you an appointment to use a special library. This is the case with the joint library of the International Monetary Fund and the International Bank for Reconstruction and Development, known also as the World Bank.

However, short of such privileges, you may circumvent these barriers by enlisting the help of a librarian in a library other than the one to which you are trying to gain access. Having a librarian contact the special library of your choice effectively establishes your credibility. This strategy has helped even people who wanted to use the libraries of area law and consulting firms. "Some of these organizations will allow you to use their collections if they do not see you as competition in the marketplace and feel you have a legitimate research need that other libraries cannot fill," one librarian says. To learn about area law libraries' holdings, consult the *Union List of Legal Periodicals* published by the Law Librarians' Society of Washington, D.C. The book also lists the rules of access, phone numbers, and locations of 185 academic, government, and private law libraries that are members of the Society.

Before you make an appointment at a special library, make sure its holdings really meet your research needs by checking the directories listed in the box on page 54. Calling various libraries about their holdings may also be helpful, especially if there are several libraries collecting materials in the same field. The directories also give up-to-date information on access regulations.

A library's holdings may be listed as books, trade and professional journals, technical reports, and congressional and regulatory agency hearings. Entries listing "vertical files" may lead to virtual treasures of clippings and pamphlets on designated topics. Some special libraries have materials outside the federal domain, such as transcripts of hearings before state agencies, but others leave it to their state chapters to collect data on states, regions, and cities. In some cases, special libraries also contain an organization's archives. This is less common for an entity of the federal government, where records tend to be stored in the National Archives. However, some agencies keep records in a separate archive frequently connected to the History Office. Storage in a History Office Archive usually provides easier access than storage in the National Archives.

Special libraries may offer some materials easily available elsewhere, but much of their holdings cannot be found in other libraries. The library of the American Society of Association Executives (ASAE) is a case in point. "There just is not any other library that includes extensive materials on that subject in its collection," said the manager of research and information at ASAE.

When author Paul A. Dickson researched *The Great American Ice Cream Book* in the early 1970s, he was allowed access to materials of the International Association of Ice Cream Manufacturers. "I found boxes and boxes of clippings on ice cream, some of them dating back 50 years," he said.

## Government Libraries

Similarly, holdings of government libraries support the programs of a given agency or department. This means the main library at the Department of Commerce provides national and international information on business, economics, marketing, and industry, while the reference library at the Small Business Administration addresses similar topics with specific emphasis on small firms.

When conducting research be aware that resource centers and public document rooms may provide you with some unpublished documents or with more current materials than libraries. In addition, there may be more than one library in a federal department. In the Department of Commerce, for example, there are several major libraries maintained by agencies within the department (National Bureau of Standards Library; Patent and Trademark Office Scientific Library; Bureau of the Census Library).

Conducting research in a government library may require more effort than working in a public library, because budget cuts and staff reductions are taking their toll. Even in federal libraries, where once you could count on assistance, the friendly librarian may not have time to be so friendly anymore.

Among the federal libraries are the National Agricultural Library in Beltsville, Maryland, with a branch in the Department of Agriculture downtown; and the National Library of Medicine, in Bethesda, Maryland. Both serve the personnel of the departments that maintain them and the public with on-site use of materials.

The National Agricultural Library is the largest agricultural library in the world with mostly scientific and technical holdings of approximately 1.7 million volumes in 1982. Because much of it is stored on closed stacks, you should schedule enough time for your visit. However, users do have quick access to the extensive reference collection in the main reading room and to the 800 journals with issues for the current calendar year on display in the periodical reading room.

The National Library of Medicine is a component of the National Institutes of Health. NIH, which is the principal medical research arm of the federal government, is a part of the U.S. Department of Health and Human Services. (See also "Health and Medicine," page 83.)

The National Library of Medicine is the world's largest reference center devoted to a single scientific subject. The library's collection includes approximately three million items, covering books, journals, theses, audiovisuals (tapes and films), manuscripts, and photographs. The holdings do not include any of the pamphlets or brochures NIH publishes to educate the public; these are available from the public information offices of the various NIH institutes.

The library is open to the public for on-site use, although some of the materials are available through interlibrary loan. In most general terms, the library divides its holdings into a collection on the history of medicine and a general collection. The former includes manuscripts, books, and photographs up to 1870; the latter includes approximately 24,000 journals. Access is gained through the on-line catalog, which covers materials acquired and processed since 1965. Arranged by subject and author, the catalog allows a free search of the library's holdings.

To become more familiar with the library, request from the public affairs office the free booklets *The National Library of Medicine* (general information) and the *National Library of Medicine Users Guide*, which discusses services and collections. There is also a tour that starts at the Lister Hill Center Building daily at 1 p.m. Groups must call ahead for tour reservations.

Given the magnitude of the collection in the National Library of Medicine and the closed stacks, you may find it easier to get some material at the National Institutes of Health Library or the National Institutes of Mental Health Library. Both have open stacks, which allow you easier access; the NIH library also offers a daily tour. However, unlike the National Library of Medicine, both these libraries serve primarily their departments' personnel.

## Folger Shakespeare Library

*201 East Capitol Street, SE, Washington, DC 20003*

One of Washington's unexpected pleasures is the Folger Shakespeare Library. While tourists know it as the place to gaze at a representation of the Globe Theatre and other artifacts from the time of the Bard, and Washington residents patronize its excellent acting company, scholars appreciate it as a treasure of Renaissance lore. The library itself operates under the trusteeship of Amherst College, and its use is restricted to scholars with the requisite credentials. For those academicians, what awaits is the world's largest collection of Shakespeareana. More than a quarter-million volumes reflect works relating not just to Shakespeare and his time, but to all of Renaissance Europe. The Folger now owns nearly 60 percent of all known books printed in English before 1640.

The Folger seems an unlikely neighbor of the Capitol. It stands in the federal city because oil magnate Henry Clay Folger, whose private collection formed the foundation of the present holdings, wanted his books to be close to the Library of Congress, and, according to Washington writer E.J. Applewhite, Folger's wife liked the city. Scholars of the period (and not only those doing work on Shakespeare) must be eternally grateful.

## Public Libraries

Public library systems serve everyone and, in the Washington area, several systems are available. Metropolitan library systems share resources in a number of ways, balancing the differences in holdings caused by various levels of funding. Most convenient for patrons is the reciprocal borrowing agreement through which anyone with a card in library System A may borrow books from library System B and return them at System A or any other participating systems. Sometimes you may use the actual borrower's card from System A in System B; in other cases, a new card will be issued. Participating in the reciprocal agreement are the District of Columbia, Alexandria, Falls Church, and Arlington, Fairfax, Loudoun, Montgomery, Prince George's, and Prince William's counties, according to the Metropolitan Washington Library Council, which initiated the program.

Also helpful is the speedy interlibrary loan service called Library Express. It delivers materials within 24 hours between the more than 100 branches of seven public libraries and the library of George Mason University. Participating are Arlington, Fairfax, Loudoun, Montgomery, Prince George's and Prince William's counties and the city of Alexandria.

To use the situation to your advantage, you need to learn about the strengths in holdings in each library system, including the special collections. You may use various guidebooks and verify the information with the administrative offices of a given system, if necessary. Library systems also publish brochures about special holdings, which include the Noyes Library for children's books in Montgomery County and the Selima Room in the Bowie Branch of the Prince George's library system, which houses materials on horse breeding and racing, with emphasis on Maryland horses.

However, the quickest way to use area library resources is by telephone. You may pick up the free brochure *ASK US* at a local library; it lists the phone numbers of the reference desks in every branch of the metropolitan library systems. The brochure was published by the Metropolitan Washington Library Council. As a rule, a telephone inquiry should be a question that lends itself to a quick answer with the use of standard reference tools. Librarians generally keep you on the line while they find the answer, but some are willing to call you back.

The telephone reference in the Martin Luther King Memorial Library of the District of Columbia is a time saver for Washington writers. This is the place to call if you want to know how many politicians preceded Helmut Schmidt in his post as the chancellor of the Federal Republic of Germany or if roaches have teeth (they do, in a technical sense). If you have a more specialized question, you may want to contact the reference librarian in a given subject division of the library. However, if you want to know about library holdings, services, facilities, or programs, call Book Information.

Within Martin Luther King Memorial Library, the Washingtoniana Division and the *Washington Star* Collection may well offer the most useful tools for a writer. The *Washington Star* Collection contains the former newspaper's morgue and photo library donated to the library after the *Star* closed. The collection contains approximately 13 million clippings arranged by subject and personal name, covering international, national, and local news starting in the 1930s. Each *Star* article was clipped and placed in as many different files as necessary to cover all topics or personal names mentioned in it, librarians say. Also in the collection are more than one million photographs, arranged by subject and personal name, covering international, national, and local news. You may make arrangements to buy copies of some photographs, although many of them are copyrighted. When looking for illustrations, consider the library's separate picture collection, which is loaned to the public. The *Star* Collection includes the newspaper's archives, which detail its history. (See also page 76.)

The library's Washingtoniana Division is considered a formidable collection of historical and current materials about the development and affairs of Washington. It was begun in 1905 and contains books, periodicals, vertical files, and images of the city. All materials are for on-site use only, but open shelves encourage browsing. You will find books on the social, economic, political, and cultural history of Washington, a considerable number of assessment and real estate directories, as well as a complete set of city directories for 1822 to 1973. The vertical files contain newspaper and magazine clippings, pamphlets, and brochures arranged by subject. There are also archival collections of records from organizations as varied as the National Ballet and the League of Women Voters.

The Washingtoniana Division also houses publications of the government of the District of Columbia to a greater extent than do other area libraries. The set of agency publications and federal documents bearing on District affairs is not complete, despite the library's status as an official repository.

## University Libraries

Separate from public and special libraries are the academic

libraries maintained by area colleges and universities, which are sometimes called "Consortium of Universities of the Washington Metropolitan Area." The group consists of nine libraries, which have holdings of more than 5.5 million volumes, 3.5 million items on microform, and 62,000 serial subscriptions.

Access to these resources is meant primarily for faculty members and students of the universities, which may maintain law and health sciences libraries in addition to general collections. Outsiders are generally permitted on-site use of materials in the general libraries, but not in the special libraries. You may be required to show identification when entering a library, as is the case at George Washington's Gelman Library. With identification you will get a pass allowing library use for that day. However, rules are set by each individual institution; the group consists of American University, the Catholic University of America, Gallaudet College, George Washington University, Georgetown University, Howard University, Mount Vernon College, Trinity College, and the University of the District of Columbia.

To be entitled to other benefits, including borrowing privileges, you generally have to join a Friends of the Library or Library Associates program. This may be as reasonable as $15 at Catholic University and Georgetown University or as high as $100 at George Washington University. However, permanent Georgetown residents can get a borrower's card at Georgetown University because they live in the university's neighborhood. Georgetown's long library hours are an extra bonus.

Holdings of the libraries are described in the respective directories and also in a free brochure *Guide to Library Resources* published by the Consortium. In addition to the holdings, the booklet describes the location of each library, the relevant telephone numbers, names of head librarians, parking facilities, and public transportation access.

Although most university libraries provide access to computer data bases for bibliographic searches, they limit the service to faculty members and students. The exceptions are American University, Gallaudet College, Catholic University, and Paul Himmelfarb Health Science Library of George Washington. At Catholic, a search can be performed only if the patron has a borrower's card, which outsiders can get as Friends of the Library. University libraries use data bases prepared by commercial vendors, which cover more subjects than those in use at the Library of Congress. However, the number of data bases available differs, as does the fee the user will be charged. To compare available online search services, consult the 1983 edition of the *On-line Directory: Search Services Available in Metropolitan Washington.*

Whether you are a resident writer or a visitor here on assignment, you're bound to find Washington's research facilities impressive. The documents are here in abundance, often housed in great splendor. Armed with this guide and a willingness to ask questions, most writers will find using the city's libraries and archives a pleasure.

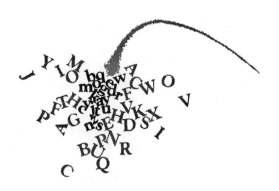

# Photo Files

## Sara Day

**Y**ears ago, when I was a picture researcher for a London weekly magazine, it was common practice to replace perfectly acceptable copy with a late-breaking, dramatic photograph. The old adage is apt: a picture's worth a thousand words. Many successful writers, however, have also found that by submitting a well-chosen photograph with their manuscript, they can do much to prejudice a busy editor in their favor. Fortunately for those who want or need to try this tactic, Washington offers millions of pictures requiring some effort but little money to obtain.

Washington is recognized by publishers and "picture people" as the United States' greatest source of public domain, i.e., out of copyright, pictures through its vast government picture archives. Besides photographs, reproducible visual images may include photographed prints, old book illustrations, paintings, posters, maps, sculpture, cartoons, invitations, manuscripts—indeed any of the memorabilia that have collected, for example,

---

*Sara Day is a freelance writer and picture researcher who, having practiced her complementary crafts in London, Philadelphia, Geneva, and Paris, is now based in Washington where she specializes in the arts and the history of many disciplines.*

in the nation's attic, the Smithsonian. Photographic archives may also be found in the capital's many private libraries and museums, trade associations, corporate lobbying offices, medical research centers, university archives, concert halls and theatres, and philanthropic organizations.

## Freelance Picture Researching

There is no reason why you should not be able to find illustrations for your own work if you're in town and have the time. Otherwise, there is a pool of professional picture researchers, members of a still small and little-known profession, who have made it their business to know the maze of picture sources in Washington. These researchers also draw on picture sources across America and internationally. Some picture researchers work fulltime for Washington area publishers, including the National Geographic Society, the Smithsonian Institution Press, Time-Life Books, and the National Wildlife Federation, and for magazines, newspapers, TV stations, and government or private organizations producing illustrated publications or exhibits. The rest are freelance, working for any of the above or for publishers in New York, London, or elsewhere.

Freelance picture researchers generally work for an hourly or daily rate ($15 to $20 an hour or about $125 to $200 a day), and are usually given a picture budget to work with. In Washington, researchers tend to focus on government archives. While archives such as the Library of Congress Prints and Photographs Division and the Still Photos Division of the National Archives provide photographs for no more than a print fee, both sources require order forms.

If you plan to order photos often, you may want to open deposit accounts rather than pay for each order separately. Processing time can vary from two to eight weeks—ask the photoduplication staff for a current time estimate. To expedite matters, place a RUSH order (usually double charge) and pick up photos rather than wait for the mail. Photos are not sent on approval, as they are by commercial stockhouses, and beyond the simplest of requests, government archives won't respond to picture lists. This means doing your own research, including careful noting of caption material since it will *not* appear on the print you receive. Also, most government archives are far stronger in black and white material than color. Fortunately, the potential for finding previously unpublished photos is higher, and the print is yours to keep with no extra charge for further uses.

## The Serious Business of Copyright

A researcher using government picture archives must be alert to the copyright of photographs. Photograph copyright is a very complex subject and picture people, like writers, are perennially searching for the ultimate authority to clarify the rules. One important guideline is that, with certain exceptions, no illustration from a publication issued since 1906 may be copied without permission. Book and other published illustrations prior to 1906 may be copied and reproduced by anyone, as may government photos that were made for a particular agency by government-employed photographers, and photographs with copyrights that have long since expired. These all fall into the public domain. However, wire service photographs and works by nongovernment photographers are often included in government files and are copyrighted. Moreover, the new copyright law of 1976 gives far clearer protection to photographers than had been the case. For example, copyright now belongs to the photographer, unless there is a written agreement to the contrary (e.g., "work made for hire"), and protection lasts the life of the originator plus 50 years (instead of the old 28 years, with an option to renew for a further 28 years).

Several collections at the Library of Congress and National Archives, and much of the material in the *Washington Star* Photo Morgue contain copyrighted photographs that are unavailable for reproduction unless permission is sought from the relevant copyright holders. The safest course is to obtain written permission and pay the required fee. If the copyright holder cannot be found, it is imperative to retain written proof that a diligent search has been made. The researcher should also consider the rights of the subject of a photograph who may be protected by law if his or her image is used in a way that invades privacy, implies ridicule, or is potentially libelous. If there is any question, then it makes sense to secure a "model release."

For more information on copyright as it applies to photographs, try *General Guide to the Copyright Act of 1976*, (Library of Congress, U.S. Copyright Office, 1979) and *Photography: What's the Law?* by Robert M. Cavallo and Stuart Kahan (New York: Crown Publishers Inc., 1979).

## Pros and Cons of Commercial Sources

When using commercial stockhouses you may feel assured that the copyright status of their photos is generally straightforward. However, compared to a one-time cost of about $7 for Library of Congress prints, one pays a minimum of $75 for regular page use of black and white and $100 for color, to hundreds and even thousands of dollars for front or inside cover or advertising use, and foreign language editions. In addition, stockhouses often charge a service fee of $35 to $50 for the research and a holding fee for keeping photos longer than specified—usually waived if one buys rights. These fee levels reflect stockhouses' speed of service, excellent contemporary color and black and white photography (stockhouses generally supply original material, whereas government archives often provide duplicates), in-house research, and photos sent out on approval. A cardinal rule is to clarify conditions of loan and use beforehand.

The picture researcher, picture list in hand, quickly establishes a list of sources, particularly of inexpensive or free photographs for tight budgets. Source lists may be compiled partially by studying the picture credits in books on similar subjects. A useful bibliography for finding highly illustrated books by subject is Renata Shaw's *Picture Searching: Techniques and Tools* (Special Libraries Association, 1976). Visits to Washington sources often begin with the photo divisions of the Library of Congress and National Archives.

## Library of Congress

The Prints and Photos Division of the Library of Congress is located in spacious quarters on the third floor of the James Madison Memorial Building, a marked contrast to its previous cramped location in the Library of Congress Annex. This world-wide visual record of people, places, and events numbering ten million prints, photographs, negatives, posters, and other pictorial materials, is constantly growing through bequests and acquisitions. A large body of material awaits cataloging and is thus unknown and inaccessible—a tantalizing buried treasure.

The library's photograph collection, one of the largest in the country, is arranged by subject with access through the divisional card catalog and numerous other indexes in the reading room. Important sections include Civil War photos by Mathew Brady, the Depression era conditions across rural America in the Farm Security Administration, the Office of War Information collection, the Historic American Buildings Survey, and Nazi photos captured during World War II. Researchers may personally check portrait, specific subject, Farm Security Administration, and geographical files, and many others, in the reading room. For more complex needs, the curators of each division (Fine Prints, Historical Prints, Master Photographs, Architectural Collections, and Posters) will consult by appointment, and the experienced and very helpful reference staff will help all comers from Monday to Friday between 8:30 a.m. and 5 p.m. The division maintains a list of freelance picture researchers. Prints must be ordered through the library's Photoduplication Services and copy photography is allowed only under very special circumstances.

While the Prints and Photographs Division is the library's primary source of illustrations, excellent original visual material may be found in divisions such as Geography and Maps, Manuscripts, Orientalia, Rare Books, Motion Pictures, and Music. A useful and well-indexed introduction is *Special Collections in the Library of Congress* by Annette Melville (Library of Congress, 1980).

## National Archives

The Still Photos Division of the National Archives, an immensely important visual archive because it houses a huge and constantly growing collection of photographs from the inactive files of more than 130 agencies, poses particular problems to the researcher. First of all, you must apply for a research card in the lobby of the Pennsylvania Avenue entrance before being allowed access to Still Photos. Since the photos are filed by the agency of origin it is necessary to use sleuth instincts to pinpoint the likely location of a subject. There is no general catalog, although there are lists and bibliographies, including the original card catalog from each agency, if such a thing ever existed! It is a good idea here to seek out a friendly reference assistant.

Among the more interesting collections are records of the Works Projects Administration; Foreign Records Seized (including Heinrich Hoffman photos of the rise of the Nazis, and the personal photo albums of Joachim von Ribbentrop and Eva Braun); more Mathew Brady photos; the Abbie Rowe White House Collection of the FDR through the Johnson Administrations; World War II Crimes Records (Nuremburg and Tokyo); the photo morgue of the Paris Bureau of *The New York Times*, 1900-1950; the Army, Air Force, and Marine Corps photos before 1941; and Navy photos before 1958. These photographic archives have been swelled recently by the addition of the DOCU-MERICA slides of environmental conditions in the U.S. from the Environmental Protection Agency; and the archives of the Drug Enforcement Administration, Atomic Energy Commission, Bureau of Mines, and Bureau of Prisons. Particular care must be taken in checking the copyright status of photographs if they are to be reproduced. Prints and transparencies must be ordered through the National Archives photographic service or, for those who cannot wait the standard six weeks, the Archives allows researchers to copy photographs using their own cameras and lights.

As with the Library of Congress, excellent visual material may be found in many other divisions of the National Archives, particularly the Cartographic Archives Division, the Center for Polar Archives, and the Diplomatic Branch, where the illustrations are often interfiled with written material.

## Defense Audio-Visual Agency

The situation with Defense Department photos is in a state of flux, but at least the four armed services photographic archives are now located under one roof in Building 168 at the Anacostia Naval Station in Southwest Washington. The Still Media Depository Branch of the Defense Audio-Visual Agency (DAVA) will include all active Defense Department photographic material plus negatives of material in the Art Activities of each service. New research and ordering procedures are still being worked out.

DAVA staff request an appointment three days in advance and will do limited research in response to requests. However, because they will respond with a choice of three negative numbers for each subject, from which you must make a blind choice, you are better off selecting the photos personally, or hiring a researcher.

The Navy Combat Art Center, with paintings and prints of Navy activities from 1941 to the present, is located in Building 67 at the Washington Navy Yard, and the Naval Historical Center is now in Building 108. The latter is the best source of naval historical illustrations before World War II and supplements the National Archives and DAVA from World War II on. The Marine Corps Art Program is also at the Navy Yard in Building 198. The Army Art Activity in Alexandria expects to move within the area; its permanent mailing address is U.S. Army Center of Military History, Attention DAMH-HSA, 20 Massachusetts Avenue, NW, Washington, DC 20314. The Air Force Art Collection is the only one remaining at the Pentagon and may be visited by appointment. Negatives of the various art collections may usually be found at DAVA.

As for recent Coast Guard photos, they are to be found in the Coast Guard building (2100 2nd Street, SW) and their Public Affairs Division will head you toward the relevant divisions. The excellent World War II Coast Guard photos are at the National Archives.

## Smithsonian Institution and Other Museums

Another vast and multifaceted government source of pictures is the Smithsonian Institution. One has only to look at the scope of its divisions to comprehend the richness of this resource, from the National Museum of American History to the National Air and Space Museum, from the National Museum of Natural History to the various art museums. Its art museums, including the Freer, the Hirshhorn, the National Museum of American Art/ National Portrait Gallery, the Renwick, and the National Museum of African Art, offer the best sources of photos of works of art in Washington, along with the National Gallery of Art, which includes its own photographic service. Research should start in the appropriate bureau and division where subject lists and catalogs are found and curators will provide expert guidance. A notable exception is the Museum of American History, which is centralizing its visual material in its new Archives Center. Access is limited and appointments should be made with the archivists.

The Smithsonian's Office of Printing and Photographic Services in the National Museum of American History provides direct picture service for the entire institution except for the Freer Gallery, part of the National Museum of American Art, the National Portrait Gallery, and the Hirshhorn Museum, which have their own photographic services. (Once an item description and the all-important negative number are pinned down, a photographic order form should be obtained from this office.) It is mandatory to request permission to reproduce in writing, to pay for photo orders in advance, and to credit the relevant division.

Examples of aids to research to be found in each division include the National Portrait Gallery's "Illustrated Checklist of the Permanent Collection," containing miniature reproductions of each portrait, documentation, and negative number, and their Catalog of American Portraits (CAP) which keeps a central record of photographs and documentation of American portraits in public and private collections throughout the country. You may not order photos through CAP but rather must apply to the owner of the portrait in question. The National Museum of American Art houses the computerized "Bicentennial Inventory of American Paintings Executed before 1914," an extremely valuable study collection of photos and reproductions. A specialized cross-divisional research guide is the *Finder's Guide to Prints and Drawings in the Smithsonian Institution* by Linda Corey Claassen (Smithsonian Press, 1981).

The Smithsonian offers much more than photos of artwork. Researchers may order color photos of historic advertisements, greeting cards, and product packages, for example, from the National Museum of American History's Warshaw Collection of Business Americana. One may also acquire photos of three-dimensional items from Smithsonian collections, ranging from an Amish quilt to a McCormick reaper.

Research at the National Gallery should begin by studying its numerous published catalogs. Acquisition numbers serve as negative numbers and should be noted with the artist and full title in a written request to the Office of Photographic Services. Black and white photographs must be prepaid and color transparencies are rented for three months. The Gallery is firm about correct usage and faithful reproduction and asks to see color proofs before publication. As for private art galleries, in the case of the Corcoran gallery it is necessary to approach the Registrar, and the Phillips Collection has photographs of most of its holdings.

## Guides to Picture Sources

There are so many specialized photographic archives in Washington that it is only appropriate to name a few here. Those interested in taking this subject further might consult *Pictorial Resources in the Washington, D.C. Area* by Shirley L. Green and Diane Hamilton (Library of Congress, 1976). This information-packed bible of the industry is already somewhat out of date (the fate of all government reference books) but can be purchased for $5.75 plus $2 handling charges prepaid from the Library of Congress Information Office, Box A, Washington, DC 20540. Another picture researcher's bible, with a valuable introduction to the techniques and tools of picture researching, is *Picture Sources 3* by Ann Novotny and Rosemary Eakins, a 1975 publication of the Special Libraries Association, which, as it is out of print, must be consulted in libraries. *World Photography Sources*, by David N. Bradshaw and Catherine Hahn (Directories, 1982) gives an update on names, addresses, and telephone numbers, has a useful introduction on "Researcher Guidelines," but is sketchy in its source descriptions and expensive ($42).

## Library Photo Archives

Some of the best picture archives in the area are maintained by libraries: federal (the National Library of Medicine), public (Martin Luther King Memorial Library), university (Georgetown University Library) or private (Folger Shakespeare Library and Dumbarton Oaks). The History of Medicine Division of the National Library of Medicine in Bethesda maintains a fine graphics collection on the history of medicine, portraits, and medical subjects, including an exceptional collection of cartoons, all of which are available through a subject card catalog. Many of the images have been photographed from rare book illustrations resulting from original research in the Rare Books Division, and you can have any new discoveries photographed by its weekly visiting photographic service for the cost of a print.

The Arts, Audiovisual, and Washingtoniana divisions of the Martin Luther King Memorial Library have photos and tearsheets arranged in subject files. Much of this material is intended for reference purposes rather than for reproduction (although the Washingtoniana Division has negatives of Washington historical material), but the library will soon offer an important new source of reproducible photos of local, national, and international subjects, through the recently acquired photo morgue of the defunct *Washington Star*. This promises exciting possibilities when it is made generally available and is already useful for reference purposes.

Another source for local historical illustrations such as photos, engravings, lithographs, and woodcuts of downtown and northwest Washington is the Columbia Historical Society. The Special Collections Division of Georgetown University Library has a considerable archive of black and white photos and some transparencies both on university life and history and on such subjects as the Washington political scene, the American motion picture industry, and railroads. George Washington University's Gelman Library also has an interesting photo archive. One of the best illustrations card catalogs in Washington is located at the Folger Shakespeare Library, where librarians have cataloged by subject the illustrations in all their folio size books printed before 1641, and some quarto books. They are working on books printed between 1641 and 1700. There is also an arts card catalog describing the Folger's prints and other works on paper, and a photograph catalog. Since their books range far beyond the subject of Shakespeare, it is worth checking the Folger's catalogs for English, European, and American history of many disciplines. Many of the images to be found there have already been photographed and the Folger is blessed with a highly efficient in-house photo lab.

Dumbarton Oaks offers illustrations for three widely divergent areas of study: Byzantine art and archaeology in their Center for Byzantine Studies; sculpture, painted pottery and textiles in their Center for Pre-Columbian Studies; and botanical and horticultural illustrations in their Garden Library.

## Other Government Agencies

Many government agencies and offices maintain specialized photographic archives for publicity purposes. Although just a few are mentioned here, a little imagination will lead you to photographs for almost any subject in Washington. ACTION, AID, the Department of the Interior's National Park Service, the National Oceanic and Atmospheric Administration and the National Environmental Satellite Service, Department of Energy, the National Aeronautics and Space Administration (excellent free black and white and loaned color), U.S. Army Corps of Engineers, FBI, U.S. Forest Service, National Arboretum (free), Department of Agriculture, National Institutes of Health (several individual institutes have their own photographic archives), House of Representatives Photography Collection, Senate Historical Office, White House Photo Office (for the current administration—free), Architect of the Capitol (see their excellent reference work, *Art in the U.S. Capitol*, Government Printing Office, 1978), Department of State, and the U.S. Customs Service are all tried and true sources of photographs. Incidentally, unless you have unusual connections, it is pointless to approach the CIA for anything more than a view of their building and rigid official portraits of past and present Directors—they're not looking for publicity.

## International Photo Sources

There are also several Washington sources for overseas subjects. It is usually worthwhile contacting the librarian, or press or cultural attache of the relevant embassy because, even if they cannot help directly, they may offer a hotline to their tourist bureaus or consulates. The European Communities Information Service, the U.N. Food and Agriculture Organization, the U.N. Information Center, which can order from its extensive photo files in New York, the World Bank, and the Organization of American States (OAS) all have photos available for loan immediately or can order others on subjects relating to their activities worldwide.

## Publicity Photos

Private sources will generally lend photographs free of charge in return for the publicity of a credit line, a fairly standard requirement, and photos are often available at once. This holds true for private philanthropic organizations such as the American National Red Cross and Project HOPE, although the National Trust for Historic Preservation does charge and orders take six weeks to process. The public information departments of performing arts centers such as the Kennedy Center, Wolf Trap Foundation, Arena Stage, American Film Institute, National Theater, and Ford's Theater, whose collection reflects its historic associations, provide photos in exchange for a credit line, sometimes free and sometimes for a print fee. The many hundreds of trade associations and trade unions headquartered in Washington are excellent sources for photos although, for obvious reasons, all of them require a credit line and many of them charge for photo processing. (Check Gale's *Encyclopedia of Associations* for names and addresses.) Public relations offices of local companies usually offer free photos for a credit line, and it is also worth trying the Washington offices of large corporations.

## Commercial Sources

As every Washington researcher knows, there comes a time when there is nothing else to do but call the wire services such as UPI or Wide World, or general photo agencies including Time-Life Picture Agency in New York. For general subjects, particularly if you need color, try Washington-area commercial stockhouses such as Uniphoto Picture Agency and Woodfin Camp in Washington, and Photri and Roloc Color Slides in Alexandria. Also check the Yellow Pages under "Photographers" or "Photographs, Stock" and the *Stock Photo and Assignment Source Book* (New York: R.R. Bowker, 1977). The commercial stockhouses will refer you to freelance photographers for special assignments as will the Washington chapter of the American Society of Magazine

Photographers and the White House News Photographers Association. Many local photographers, for example Fred Maroon, Jim Pickerell, and Paul Conklin, have impressive archives of their own stock. Although the *National Geographic* does not release any of its photographs for reproduction, its rights and permissions director will refer interested researchers to its freelance photographers. The names of freelance picture researchers in the Washington area may also be obtained from the American Society of Picture Professionals (ASPP), Box 5283, Grand Central Station, New York, NY 10017.

So now you are ready to submit several judiciously chosen, high quality illustrations with your text. Be warned that the editor, or picture editor, will want to know the exact credit line for each photograph and whether permission has been obtained in writing where required (although, if you're lucky, these mechanical details will be handled by the in-house picture people). Perhaps you will find, as other writers have, that the added visual dimension makes all the difference between being read or overlooked, accepted or rejected.

# The Writer
# As Specialist

In a city where writers are as numerous as lawyers and lobbyists, it often pays to be a specialist. While areas of specialization no doubt are limited only by one's imagination, we've chosen here to concentrate on four: "Medicine," "Business," "Education," and "Science." Each of these fields exists separately from the federal presence, but necessarily each is shaped by it. Thus Washington is seen by one writer as "heaven for a medical writer," largely because of the federal funding that supports such institutions as NIH. The business community flourishes here, but somewhat differently from the way it does in other cities. Education policy originates here, a fact that provides writers a unique view of the field. While many writers prefer to remain generalists, those who wish to specialize will find the nation's capital a fine setting for such concentration.

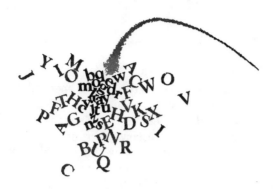

# Health and Medicine

### Elaine Blume

Washington is heaven for a medical writer. From the National Institutes of Health (NIH) in Bethesda to congressional offices on Capitol Hill, a writer covering health topics in this city is conspicuously surrounded by the best. And sources are matched by resources. The National Library of Medicine, for example, is unexcelled in its field, but if it doesn't suit a given occasion, there are five medical libraries and several public library systems to choose from in the area, as well as specialized collections maintained by private health organizations.

These organizations are another of Washington's assets. Besides maintaining libraries, they are eager to press reams of printed material into accepting hands, and they provide access to experts thoroughly conversant with who is who and what is what in their own small universes.

---

*Elaine Blume has master's degrees in medical sciences from the University of Illinois and from Harvard. She was a writer/editor at the National Institutes of Health from 1968 to 1971. Since then, she has written for the government and for magazines including* Vogue *and* Harper's Bazaar.

In little ways, too, Washington serves medical writers well. Whether you want to buy a gynecology text, join an active professional group, study biochemistry, or see for yourself what a gallstone looks like, this is a city where it can be done. If you are writing about the policy side of health, Washington is not just a good place to be—it is the only place. The Washington writer has ready access to the congressional committees and subcommittees that develop national health policies, the government agencies that carry them out, and the health lobbies that keep busy here promoting their own points of view.

On earth, though, even heaven has its flaws. Disadvantages of working as a medical writer in Washington include dealing with over-cautious bureaucrats and battling layers of government clearance in a system where any scientist's word—or whim—is likely to be law, with regard to prose style as well as technical substance.

The medical writer in Washington is apt to find NIH at the center of his or her working life. This "jewel in the crown" of the federal health effort boasts some 2,000 top-notch medical researchers, including several Nobel laureates, an outstanding research hospital, two large and numerous small libraries, and a number of offices specifically devoted to dispensing information.

NIH's research hospital, or Clinical Center, and many of its offices and labs are located on 306 acres in Bethesda. But portions of the agency are scattered throughout suburban Maryland and as far afield as North Carolina, Montana, and overseas.

The NIH is a wonderful place to sniff around for story ideas, whether on your own or guided by helpful information personnel. It's the perfect place for keeping yourself up to date on the medical research scene, via publications like the *NIH Record*, and *News and Features*, as well as meetings and seminars listed in the "yellow calendar" of events. (There is also an unlisted series of seminars designed especially for science writers.) Most important, NIH is unbeatable as a repository for specialists in almost every conceivable area of medicine who are able—and usually willing—to supply you with exactly the quote or clarification you need to complete an article.

A helpful tool for maneuvering around NIH is the agency telephone directory. Copies are sold to the public through the

Government Printing Office, but because new editions are issued about twice a year, it isn't hard to get outdated ones free. Besides listing individual office addresses and telephone numbers, these indispensable books contain maps, outline NIH's organizational structure, and provide detailed information about services and facilities.

One thing sets NIH apart from other medical research establishments: it is a major administrative center. Only a fraction of NIH-funded investigations are conducted in-house; the remainder are carried out by scientists at institutions throughout the United States and around the world. NIH's administrators and information officers know what's going on where and can put you in touch with researchers and programs in the area of your interest.

The institutes and divisions that make up NIH have small, narrow-focus libraries that a writer may use. In addition, a full-scale medical library is located in the Clinical Center. It has long hours, open stacks, and is open to the public. However, only NIH employees may sign out books and journals.

Set off at a far end of the NIH campus is another, world-renowned medical library—the National Library of Medicine. Its collection is much larger and more complete than the Clinical Center's, and since its books and journals do not circulate, they are more likely to be there when needed. On the other hand, the NLM's closed-stack system means that, to use most books and journals, you must look up the call number, fill out a form, and then wait about ten to twenty minutes for the volume to be delivered. The most frequently used recent journals and reference books, however, are directly accessible.

NLM is the home of MEDLARS, a computer-based Medical Literature Analysis and Retrieval System. For a fee, you can use this system to conduct a literature search of your own. Or you may be able to use one of the popular bibliographies that NLM reprints and distributes free of charge. A list of available titles may be obtained from the library; it also appears each month in both the complete and abridged versions of *Index Medicus.*

Remember the resources of the local medical schools. All of the area medical schools (four in Washington and two in Baltimore) maintain public relations offices, issue press releases, and will gladly add your name to their mailing lists. Johns Hopkins and Georgetown are especially active in suggesting story ideas. Seminars and conferences at the schools may also offer leads, along with education and the opportunity to make useful personal contacts.

The medical schools all have libraries, too. These are open to the public, and Georgetown will even extend borrowing privileges to an outsider, for a fee.

Washington medical writers are likely to go to NIH with some frequency, visit a medical school occasionally, and get out every so often for an interview elsewhere. But much of their time, like that of most journalists, is spent shut up in a room with a typewriter (or its high tech equivalent) and a telephone. During these hours, too, Washington is a good place to be. Apart from the details of research projects conducted elsewhere, almost any information a health writer could want is available here via a local call.

On the public side, places you are likely to call frequently include the Food and Drug Administration, the National Center for Health Statistics, and the Washington office of the Centers for Disease Control. I have found FDA's press office, in particular, unfailingly courteous, well-informed, and prompt in responding to queries.

In the private sector, the range of organizations is startling. Answers to questions about anything from eye care to problems of the nursing profession may be gleaned from a call to the appropriate association.

Supplementing telephone contacts with occasional visits can also be rewarding. I discovered and purchased an invaluable listing of medical schools, with addresses and telephone numbers, at the Association of American Medical Colleges; have used the well-stocked library of the American Psychological Association to research an article on phobias; and once spent a memorable and productive day talking to charming elder sportsmen at the President's Council on Physical Fitness and Sports.

A health writer's work is, in itself, educational. But because medicine is so complex, you may find that you prefer to learn some things in a classroom instead of on the job. Local colleges and universities, of course, offer day and evening classes in a variety of subjects. But the part-time student of science may find his needs better met by one of two very special area institutions: the Foundation for Advanced Education in the Sciences, located on the NIH campus, and the Department of Agriculture's Graduate School. Each maintains a bookstore and offers a wide range of evening courses.

A notable feature of Washington is its great museums, several of which deserve a medical writer's attention. The Museum of Natural History, along with other parts of the Smithsonian, and the Armed Forces Medical Museum at Walter Reed Hospital, offer the health writer inspiration as well as a unique way of learning.

Finally, medical writers in Washington know they are not alone. In addition to Washington Independent Writers, which represents and serves the full range of freelance writers, this city boasts active chapters of the American Medical Writers Association, the National Association of Science Writers, and the Society for Technical Communication. These organizations sponsor workshops, speakers, tours, and other forms of continuing education; keep members informed of scheduled events and relevant news; serve as clearinghouses for jobs; and represent the interests of their memberships in Congress and elsewhere. Most important, they provide Washington health writers with opportunities to meet their peers—men and women who, like themselves, are plying a difficult trade in a city that demands the best.

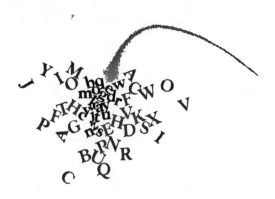

# Business

## Lisa Berger

In a place where politics is generally presumed to be the only game in town, it may come as a surprise that the world of business provides a rich field for writers. While the other members of the press corps are dogging politicians, the business writer has the rest of the city, not to mention the suburbs, wide open. And while financial and business writers (they're lumped together here) rarely receive invitations to shrimp-laden receptions or get to dig into the shadowy pasts of public officials, they may discover ample opportunity to profile companies or executives, to report on tax laws and rulings, to tell of trends in industries heavily regulated from Washington, and to write about investment strategies and specific business activities.

Some business writers in Washington follow breaking news, such as the passage of tax legislation or reporting on newly released economic figures. But business writing here gets meatier

*Lisa Berger, a freelance writer for more than ten years, specializes in the areas of energy and business. Her stories have covered the stock market, personal investing, and energy workers. She has written for national magazines, presidential commissions, and private companies.*

the further you move from the federal government. Government is a source of statistics and information, but usually not the heart of a business story. The various agencies produce reams of studies and testimony that can add national scope and authority to a local issue or confirm business developments or points of view.

Federal offices that generate background information include: Securities and Exchange Commission, Internal Revenue Service, Federal Reserve Board, Bureau of Labor Statistics, Federal Trade Commission, Commodities Futures Trading Commission, Consumer Product Safety Commission, Export-Import Bank, Small Business Administration, National Labor Relations Board, Occupational Safety and Health Administration, Federal Communications Commission, and the list could go on. The point is, before plunging in, check for a government agency that may be regulating, investigating, or studying the subject of your story.

On Capitol Hill, a committee or subcommittee may have held hearings or published studies on a particular issue or business problem. In addition to the committees (see the *Congressional Staff Directory* for the individual names), other Hill sources are the Office of Technology Assessment, Congressional Budget Office and ad hoc commissions that are created to investigate an issue and make recommendations to Congress. *The U.S. Government Manual* lists these commissions.

So much for government's role in business writing. Hundreds of industry groups in the city provide another valuable resource. These associations exist not only to lobby Congress and the White House, but also to disseminate information about their business and members. Some of these associations are veritable institutions—The U.S. Chamber of Commerce, National Association of Manufacturers, American Petroleum Institute, and American Banking Association, to name a few.

For virtually any business story, there is an association or trade group following the same issue. For instance, before talking to companies for a story on how the consulting business was faring under Ronald Reagan, I unearthed the Professional Services Council. And, for an article on the burgeoning business of financial newsletters, I located the National Association of Newsletters.

Two sources are helpful in finding a relevant industry group.

---

## Making Sense Out of Dollars

With the economy among the top stories of the decade, focus has turned to a handful of previously obscure government departments and agencies, many of which play a major role in interest rates, government fiscal policy, and other aspects of the American—and world—economy. All of these organizations provide writers with valuable information resources on all aspects of banking, finance, and economics.

Here is a representative sampling:

**Bureau of Economic Analysis,** Department of Commerce, 1401 K Street, NW, Washington, DC 20230; 202/523-0777. Provides statistical data on economic activity, gross national product, income, industrial production, balance of payments, and a myriad of other economic indicators.

**Bureau of Labor Statistics,** 441 G Street, NW, Washington, DC 20212; 202/523-1913. Provides a wealth of data on employment figures, consumer price indexes, and other monthly economic data.

**Congressional Budget Office,** House Annex #2, U.S. Congress, Washington, DC 20515; 202/226-2621. Provides research and analysis for Congress on federal budget matters.

**Council of Economic Advisors,** Old Executive Office Building,

---

The American Society of Association Executives has a library and staff familiar with other associations, and Gale's *Encyclopedia of Associations* lists all associations in the country. Washington has more associations than any other American city. (See also chapter on "Lobbying," page 31.)

Special interest publications are another source for stories about an industry. Industry newsletters contain market reports, technology and patent information, news of executive changes, and financial results. McGraw-Hill, for instance, publishes over a dozen letters, such as *Coal Week, Nucleonics Week,* and *Platt's Oilgram News.* Other industry letters include *Defense Week, Energy Daily, Air/Water Pollution Report, Food Transport Week, Daily Tax Report, Blue Chip Economic Indicators,* and dozens more. The best places to find a newsletter on your subject are

Washington, DC 20500; 202/395-5042. This is the president's inner circle of economic gurus.

**Federal Reserve System,** Board of Governors, 20th Street and Constitution Avenue, NW, Washington, DC 20551; 202/452-3204. The "Fed" plays a major role in influencing interest rates and money supply, and regulates its member banks.

**General Accounting Office,** 441 G Street, NW, Washington, DC 20548; 202/275-2812. The investigative arm of Congress, GAO provides legal, accounting, and auditing services on financial and other matters.

**Joint Economic Committee,** G133 Dirksen Senate Office Building, Washington, DC 20510; 202/224-5171. The principal congressional office on economic affairs.

**Office of Management and Budget,** Old Executive Office Building, Washington, DC 20500; 202/395-3080. The principal government budget office, OMB may be the only agency to understand the detailed minutiae of the federal budget.

**Securities and Exchange Commission,** 500 North Capitol Street, Washington, DC 20549; 202/272-2650. Oversees disclosure of financial and other information about companies whose securities (stocks and bonds) are offered for public sale. This is a good place to start research on almost any privately held corporation.

*—Joel Makower*

*Hudson's Washington News Media Contacts Directory* or one of several directories of newsletters.

Writing about investments (money markets, stock markets, bonds, commodities, futures) from Washington requires lots of legwork and probably multiple phone calls to New York. Besides the obvious regulatory bodies and relevant associations, primary sources of investment information are the regional brokerage houses. While all the national houses (Merrill Lynch, Paine Webber, etc.) maintain offices here, their analysts most knowledgeable about a Washington company may well be in New York. Regional brokers (Ferris & Co., Johnston, Lemon & Co., and Folger, Nolan Flemming and Douglas, for example) are better sources for analyses of a public company operating in this area.

Another contingent of investment experts is in the trust

departments of large banks, which employ specialists in equity and fixed-income accounts.

A handful of investment newsletters are published here, and generally their editors or publishers will talk about the markets they follow. Local stand-outs are *Hulbert's Financial Digest* (which tracks other financial newsletters), *Growth Stock Outlook, Penny Stock News*, and *Personal Finance.*

Basically, Washington supports four nongovernmental industries: consulting and other so-called "professional services" (including writing); computer software; communications; and services. A fifth category is more amorphous, but includes the government-created companies, which were organized and initially funded by an act of Congress and which now operate with varying degrees of autonomy. The larger companies in this group are the Federal National Mortgage Association (Fannie Mae), U.S. Postal Service, Student Loan Marketing Association (Sallie Mae), National Railroad Passenger Corporation (Amtrak), and Communications Satellite Corporation (Comsat).

Private industry can be the subject of endless business stories. A word of warning, though. Most companies, and especially those without public shareholders, are loath to divulge much beyond press release information about their finances and management practices. The business writer, stripped of the useful "public right-to-know" argument, may have little leverage in getting company officials to reveal operation details. Talking to competitors, suppliers, and industry experts may be necessary avenues for obtaining information about a tight-lipped company.

Washington consulting companies live more or less on government contracts that call for policy analysis, program evaluations, research, training, and technical assistance. Government contracts often require extensive data collection and field surveys, and these may be available to a writer. The larger consulting/professional service firms in the area are Planning Research Corporation, BDM International, American Management Systems, and Booz-Allen & Hamilton. *Commerce Business Daily* is a noteworthy source for specifics about what the government is contracting for and who is winning the contracts.

Washington's suburbs are blossoming silicon parks populated by high-tech companies. Many of these firms deliver computer software and expertise to the Department of Defense as well as to other government departments and private business. Local giants in the field are Martin Marietta and Fairchild Industries. But dozens of smaller firms are developing innovative computer systems and doing battle for a share of the market. Companies worth following are Syscon Corporation, Input Business Machines, Tesdata Systems Corporation, Atlantic Research Corporation, and Computer Data Systems Inc.

The communications industry encompasses both news organizations and companies dealing in systems technology. *The Washington Post*, MCI Communications, *USA Today, National Geographic*, Bureau of National Affairs, Commerce Clearinghouse, and *U.S. News and World Report* fall into this category.

The Washington service industry is a melange of companies serving the affluent metropolitan area and/or national markets. Marriott Corporation, Giant Food, Woodward & Lothrop, W. Bell & Co., Peoples Drug Stores Inc., U.S. Air, GEICO, and Hechinger Company can generate stories on retailing, restaurants, airlines, hardware, and insurance.

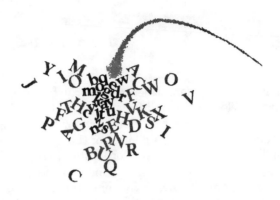

# Education
## Millie Riley

The education writer in Washington lacks not—in source, resource, idea, or material. Here, Congress develops education legislation and oversees it. The Department of Education processes and administers programs covering every aspect of instruction and learning, including programs for handicapped children, bilingual classes, Head Start, and financial aid for college students. But the true center of education activity in the city lies, no doubt, with the scores of major national associations representing the nation's consumers and practitioners of education.

Once, only school principals and teachers were presumed to be interested in reading about education. The audience is broader today, extending from parents to city planners. The public is tuning in to the impact of rising educational costs and to a high

*Millie Riley is the writer of a monthly public affairs newsletter for an education association in Washington and the editor of an educator's guide to professional developments and techniques in home economics. She has contributed freelance articles to* Today's Education.

tech world demanding continuing education, as well as to the blossom of educational travel.

Writers digging for a story angle may approach Washington's educational associations to their advantage. Many of these are located in a single building at One Dupont Circle, NW—including the American Association of State Colleges and Universities, the American Association of University Professors, the Council of Graduate Schools in the U.S., the Council on Post Secondary Accreditation, and the National Association of Land Grant Colleges and Universities.

Familiarity with numerous associations pays off for the education writer. There are associations of principals, curriculum specialists, teachers of all kinds, plus groups concerned with day care, childhood education, and exceptional children. Major sources are the powerful teacher organization, the National Education Association (NEA), and the smaller American Federation of Teachers. Executive directors of associations are valuable for reaction or comment, and program staff may provide meaty news or connection with practitioners. Future Homemakers of America, for example, a national vocational education student organization, works with teachers, teacher educators, administrators, and young people. Potential stories emerge from its philosophies—for example, youth as peer educators, and youth as leaders and decision makers.

Education associations are often good sources of information. They are easy to find through Gale's *Encyclopedia of Associations*. It's comprehensive, gives detailed profiles, and groups the education associations together. If not available in the public library, it is in the library of the American Council on Education. The Washington office of the Education Commission of the States has a small staff, but it can supply useful information. As a source for documentation, the National Center for Education Statistics will be the education writer's right arm. On first contact, ask for the statistical information office, identifying the topic and educational level related to your query. The center's experts provide, interpret, and check data, review material for accuracy, verify facts, and make data comparisons.

Most writers know to make contacts through professional associations. Washington has its own unique education group—the Washington Education Press Association. It's one of two chapters of the National Educational Press Association of America based at Glassboro State College, New Jersey. Edpress, as it is known to members, meets monthly and holds an annual workshop. Its makeup is still primarily communications staff of area education journals, but freelance members are growing in number. It makes annual awards of excellence to education periodicals and men and women responsible for them. Writers in the broadcast media may find Broadcast Education Association a source, in addition to the Association for Educational Communications and Technology, both in Washington.

*The Federal Staff Directory* will help unlock the intricacies of the Department of Education's organization and structure. It provides names and telephone numbers for a beginning contact, whether one wants to research general financial management, bilingual education and minority affairs, museum services, teacher centers, concerns of the handicapped, or adult learning. You will want to become familiar with The National Institute of Education and the National Center for Education Statistics, which are also part of the Department of Education.

National Advisory Councils are good to know. They are independent government-appointed bodies (adult education, continuing education, disadvantaged children, Indian education, vocational education, and women's educational programs). Their reports are valuable; their lists of practitioner and lay council members might be important contacts; and staff here are on the inside track of specialized education areas.

On Capitol Hill, where education legislation is written, you will frequently find highly knowledgeable congressional aides on a senator's or representative's staff, who deal exclusively with education issues. They may be useful in providing historical and back-up documentation or in securing a position statement or commentary from the legislator or committee head. In the House of Representatives, education matters fall under the jurisdiction of the Education and Labor Committee and its Subcommittee on Elementary, Secondary and Vocational Education and Subcommittee on Select Education. The U.S. Senate deals with education through its Labor and Human Resources Committee and more widely through the Subcommittee on Education, Arts, and Humanities. Hearings conducted by the committees and subcommittees may become occasions to interview educators. A list of scheduled testimony is generally available in advance. On the hearing day, the text of each presenter is available for early birds.

Some help for education writers comes from the Washington-based Council for Advancement and Support of Education (CASE). *CASE Currents*, although not a freelance outlet, is a source of ideas and leads. CASE's advice to education writers: put more of yourself into the piece and add regional color; write more about ideas.

Other specialized topical viewpoints from coalitions are useful to writers. On educational equity, one contact is the National Coalition for the Education of Women and Girls. The Committee for Education Funding is a coalition of major education organizations pooling their forces to influence education legislation.

For local school data or information, the starting point is the director of communications in the superintendent's office, D.C. Public Schools (similarly in suburban systems). On answers to questions, opinion, reaction to an action or trend, or leads to innovative programming, a grass-roots source is the D.C. Citizens for Better Public Education. Some resourceful writer will one day put together a sorely needed parents' guide to selecting schools in Washington.

In some ways Washington's education world might appear closed as a writing outlet to the independent writer. Education dailies, weeklies, and journals have their own staffs. Two once fine markets for education writers, the Department of Education's *American Education* and NEA's *Today's Education* magazines, no longer have budgets for freelance writers. They are relying on staff or on professional educators who want to be published. This has long been true for most of the journals of education associations in the Washington area. An exception is the National School Boards Association whose publication, *American School Board Journal,* is for lay people, and its *Executive Educator* for superintendents and principals. Another exception is the weekly tabloid, *Education Times,* which seeks freelance queries for features and commentary.

NEA's *Today's Education* magazine, once a quarterly, is now an annual publication. Its first edition, October 1982, was published in three versions for audiences in higher education, general education, and education support staff. It's worth it to the education writer to get a copy just for the text of 196 resolutions passed by NEA, which suggest topic ideas for any education writer. Other areas reflected in NEA publications include: educational neglect, vouchers, tax reform, rural education, environment and energy, radiation and hazardous pollution, and education rights such as pay equity, job sharing, copyright use, and tax deductions. Education touches many bases.

Editors of *The Washington Post*'s "Style Plus" section say education-focused articles are increasing. Practical how-to's for parents and education happenings with a new twist are popular topics. Writers should query first with a letter and a one-to-two paragraph outline. The newspaper has its own education news reporter who covers standard school events and school board action. But, for example, one independent writer sold "Style Plus" on a budget guide to colleges and universities; another published a piece on how to interest teenagers in reading.

Every writer must read. Daily and weekly education newsletters are briefings in themselves. They open up story leads for followup or an in-depth feature marketed to a general audience. Capitol Publications produces the leading daily, *Education Daily*. Even the U.S. Department of Education reads this one to keep up and also gives top marks to *Education Week* for its summary review. *Chronicle of Higher Education*, an independent weekly, is a respected source and relies on some 20 stringers to cover education outside Washington. It has an extensive classified section. Its library is available for reviewing back issues.

A key reference library is the Education Library of the National Institute of Education where 340 magazines and journals addressing education are accessible, as well as more than 50 newsletters, from *Education Funding News* to the *EM—The New Educational Marketer*. Many are produced in the Washington area. The library has photocopy facilities.

When you get down to writing, the *NEA Communications Style Manual* is still one of the best guides to general rules in education publications. This 19-page booklet is available free from NEA's communications division.

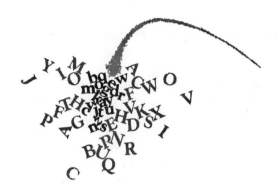

# Science

## Jane Stein

**A** gold mine of information—and publishing possibilities—exists for science writers in Washington. But it takes a bit of digging to get to the riches. Here are some ideas about what to do and where to go to tap into that mine.

**Find New Angles.** The newspapers report on scientific developments as they occur. By the time freelance writers get around to publishing a story on something new, it is in fact old. Don't try to compete with the dailies. Instead, find a new angle. When the National Academy of Sciences releases a report and it is front page news, follow up on it. Get a copy of the report, speak to the researchers who wrote it. If the findings are controversial, dig deeper into the story than a daily reporter has time to and write an investigative piece. Look for a consumer angle—for example, how will a new technology or research finding save money or lives?

---

*Jane Stein is the author of* Making Medical Choices *(Houghton Mifflin). She is a contributing editor to* National Journal *on science and health policy and is an editorial consultant to numerous private organizations and government agencies.*

**Get On Selected Mailing Lists.** Interested in aviation? Call the public information office at the National Aeronautics and Space Administration, the Federal Aviation Administration, and the Air and Space Museum. Find out what information they can send you routinely to keep you up to date. Want to cover developments in plant genetics? Call the Department of Agriculture's Research Bureau. The more specific you can be about what you are interested in covering, the better the public information office can help you by sending you information you need. Be warned: don't get on too many mailing lists or you'll be swamped with too many releases that are irrelevant to your work.

**Make Use of Government Resources.** Congress and the federal agencies make Washington a unique place for reporters. Become familiar with the activities of the House and Senate committees and subcommittees that specialize in science. A particularly good source of information for science writers is the Congressional Office of Technology Assessment, which studies the impact of energy, natural resources, materials, transportation, health, and life sciences technologies. For other science research developments, contact the National Science Foundation, the National Bureau of Standards, and the National Academy of Sciences. Although there is no one agency monitoring federal science activities, virtually every department has some science-related activities to follow—from new computerized education tools at the Department of Education to new housing technologies at the Department of Housing and Urban Development.

**Mine The Private Sector Sources, Too.** There are trade associations and public interest groups representing virtually any science issue you might want to follow. Interview researchers at local universities, laboratories, and think tanks. Another Washington specialty for reporters is former government science policy experts now working as consultants in private practice.

**Focus On Science Policy.** Since federal science policy is made in Washington, take advantage of being here by reporting on it. Take a science story (for example, new ways to test for carcinogens) and relate it to science policy. (How will this affect the standards set by the Environmental Protection Agency or the Occupational Safety and Health Administration?)

**Be Realistic.** Washington is the home of some of the best science magazines in the country: *Science, Science News, Science 83,* and *Smithsonian.* But don't bank on being published often in these magazines. Only *Science 83* and *Smithsonian* take freelance pieces regularly. The others rely exclusively on staff for articles. There are further limitations in the use of freelance science writers. Many of the articles in *Science 83* are written by staff members and contributing editors listed on the masthead. And most issues of *Smithsonian* carry proportionally few science articles: remember that the magazine covers art, history, theater, architecture, and a range of other topics as well. Don't be turned off by this realistic appraisal of Washington's science magazine market. The editors at *Science 83* and *Smithsonian* want to receive queries about good, sound science stories from local writers.

**Widen Your Horizons.** Query science magazines outside of Washington. Develop a list from *Writer's Market,* to begin, and don't limit yourself to publishing science articles in science magazines. Virtually every popular magazine includes at least one science story in each issue. Be sure to target the science story to the audience that the magazine is designed to reach.

**Look For Nonmagazine Science Writing Assignments.** Write a brochure for a federal agency, edit a report for a presidential commission or a public interest group, write speeches for officials, edit conference proceedings. There is much science writing to do in Washington. Even if it does not seem as exciting as having your name in print on a glossy magazine, it can provide interesting work. And it can lead to new story ideas that you can push—and publish—in a popular magazine.

# The Science of Science Writing

More sources and resources for science writers exist here than anywhere else in the world. Most of these resources are part of the federal government. But many others are located in private organizations, which have headquarters or branch offices here. Virtually all of them are known to be extremely helpful to writers.

## Government Sources

**Library of Congress,** Reference Section, Science & Technology Division, fifth floor, Adams Building, 2nd Street and Independence Avenue, SE, Washington, DC 20540; 202/287-5580.

**National Science Foundation,** 1800 G Street, NW, Washington, DC 20550; 202/357-9498 or 9499. This government agency provides research grants to universities.

**National Library of Medicine,** 8600 Rockville Pike, Bethesda, MD 20205; 301/496-6308. Collects and makes available medical research information.

**National Aeronautics and Space Administration,** 400 Maryland Avenue, SW, Washington, DC 20546; 202/755-8370.

**National Institutes of Health,** 9000 Rockville Pike, Bethesda, MD 20205; 301/496-4461.

**National Bureau of Standards,** Gaithersburg, MD 20234; 301/921-3112. Information on a wide spectrum of physics and technology research.

**Committee on Science and Technology,** U.S. House of Representatives, Room 2321, Rayburn House Office Building, Washington, DC 20515; 202/225-6371.

**Subcommittee on Science, Technology, and Space,** U.S. Senate, Room 251, Senate House Office Building, Washington, DC 20510; 202/224-8172.

**Congressional Office of Technology Assessment** (OTA), 600 Pennsylvania Avenue, SE, Washington, DC 20510; 202/226-2115. Reports on surveys and studies conducted for the Congress on scientific questions of wide public concern.

**Nongovernment Sources**
  **National Academy of Sciences,** 2101 Constitution Avenue, NW, Washington, DC 20418; 202/334-2142. Information on science policies, international science, advanced research in all sciences.
  **American Medical Association,** Washington Office, 1101 Vermont Avenue, NW, Washington, DC 20005; 202/789-7400. Small medical research library available with back issues of publications.
  **American Chemical Society,** 1155 16th Street, NW, Washington, DC 20036; 202/872-4450. Largest science organization in the world dedicated to one branch of science. More than 100,000 members. Large chemical research library and computerized information service.
  **Chemical Manufacturers Association,** 2501 M Street, NW, Washington, DC 20037; 202/887-1100. Industry organization. Publishes monthly *Chemecology* with research news. Makes available information on chemical research.
  **American Association for the Advancement of Science,** 1776 Massachusetts Avenue, NW, Washington, DC 20036 (also has a building at 1515 Massachusetts Avenue, NW); 202/467-4400. Largest multi-disciplinary science organization in the world, with 150,000 members. Publishes *Science* magazine and *Science 83*.
  **Atomic Industrial Forum Inc.,** 1747 Pennsylvania Avenue, NW, Suite 1150, Washington, DC 20006; 202/654-9260. Disseminates information about nuclear industry.
  **National Science Teachers Association,** 1742 Connecticut Avenue, NW, Washington, DC 20009; 202/328-5800.
  **The Association of Science-Technology Centers,** 1016 16th NW, Washington, DC 20036; 202/452-0655. Association of directors of science museums.

*—Walter Froehlich*

*Walter Froehlich's byline articles have appeared in hundreds of newspapers and magazines in scores of nations. He was for 18 years science editor of the U.S. Information Agency. He now runs his own feature service, International Science Writers, in Washington.*

# The Writer As
# Entrepreneur

The business of writing, as opposed to the craft, requires a knowledge of such practical matters as contracts, agents, lawyers, copyrights, and, ultimately, taxes. Familiarity with the tools of the trade—the books, the magazines, the publishers, the organizations and courses—smooths the way for the professional. This section begins with "The Business Side of Writing," a look at the nuts and bolts of running a small business—what one of our writers called a "cottage industry"—effectively. "Publishers" outlines a flourishing industry whose breadth may surprise those who assume that Washington publishes mainly government reports. "Publications," too, reveals a lively and varied world of magazines and journals. "Bookstores" offers writers a look at both general and specialized sources of material. Finally, "Writers' Courses" and "Writers' Organizations" explore two excellent means through which a writer maintains skills and contacts.

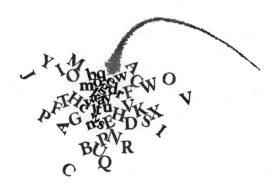

# The Business Side
# of Writing

## Suzan Richmond

*Authors are perfect patsies because they write for love.*
—Richard Curtis, literary agent.

**L**ove, however, doesn't pay the rent—or even keep you in Wite-Out. Contrary to myth, independent writers are more likely to be out hustling for assignments or selling their product than composing blank verse in some drafty Dupont Circle garret. Freelance writers who want a balanced checkbook can't afford to see themselves as anything but professional.

Still, whether you live from hand to mouth or have a fat book advance accruing interest in the bank, your one-person shop often needs services from other professionals. To stay successfully self-employed, you need to recognize that you're running a small business and discover, if you haven't, the people and organizations in Washington that will help you run it more smoothly.

The services mentioned are both obvious (legal and insurance plans set up exclusively for writers) and obscure (a hotline number to query a grammar expert about such matters as when

---

*Suzan Richmond is a Washington writer who has contributed to several books, national magazines, and newspapers. She works part-time on the staff of* Changing Times Magazine *and does freelance work.*

to use "who" or "whom"). With such resources, you may dig up business and tax advice, lawyers, insurance policies, grants, office space, word processors, answering and mailing services, and more.

## Setting Up Shop

Beryl Benderly, a Washington writer with two books and many major articles to her credit, approaches her work with a jaunty air of realism. "I think of myself as an artisan in my little cottage industry," she says, underscoring a writer's need to function competently in the business world as well as in the world of letters.

One or more of the following groups may be helpful in organizing your business as a writer. (See also groups listed under "Writers' Courses," page 142 and "Writers' Organizations," page 154.)

The Small Business Administration (1111 18th Street, NW) is a good place to begin. Ask for the package of basic information: a list of free publications (covering such topics as setting fees and sharing computer time); an information directory with numbers of referral services for lawyers, accountants, and organizations that will help you set yourself up in business without charge; and a calendar listing workshops held throughout the area on all aspects of beginning or running a business.

Writers may also get free counseling at the Small Business Development Center (2361 Sherman Avenue, NW), sponsored jointly by the Small Business Administration and Howard University. If you've been thinking about incorporating, the Center offers advice, and if you should need further expertise, you'll be referred to specialists.

While most law school clinics charge clients, the Small Business Clinic at George Washington University's National Law Center (2000 L Street, NW) is a notable exception. The only requirement is that you own or plan to own a small business. And writers qualify. The best way to get free services from a third-year law student is to plan ahead and schedule an appointment early in a semester. Legal advice is available for routine business matters like organizing corporations and drafting contracts.

# Getting Advice on Taxes

One CPA estimates that a self-employed individual is about three times more likely than a salaried worker to have his or her tax returns audited. An IRS spokesman contends such estimates can't be verified. Either way, at tax time a self-employed writer must have scrupulous records to take advantage of all legitimate deductions. Yet the tax laws on home office deductions change periodically. So do tax credits and codes. How can you master IRS forms?

If your income is low and your business expenses straightforward, you can probably figure out the intricacies of the latest tax laws yourself. Begin with the source. Call, write, or stop in at your local IRS office and ask for a free copy of Publication 334, *Tax Guide for Small Businesses*. The 168-page booklet applies both to fulltime freelance writers and to those who supplement their income by writing part-time. The inside back cover of the guide mentions other free IRS publications, such as Publication 583, on record keeping for small businesses. Local IRS offices will answer specific questions and give free advice all year round. The best time to make an appointment is early in the January to April filing season, or even earlier.

To learn more about paying your taxes, attend any one of several seasonal seminars or workshops on tax problems designed for freelance writers. Steve Kronzek, the CPA whose accounting firm handles finances for Washington Independent Writers, is usually asked to conduct an annual workshop on tax guidelines at no cost to WIW members. Nonmembers pay a nominal fee. Editorial Experts Inc. in Alexandria customarily invites an attorney to give a half-day tax and legal seminar each December; the cost is about $45. The Cultural Alliance of Greater Washington is another source of reasonably-priced information on business practices for freelance writers. "What Every Artist Should Know About Taxes But Didn't Know What To Ask" was one workshop the Cultural Alliance sponsored.

Perhaps you're beyond the do-it-yourself stage: you'd rather pay for someone else's expertise than run yourself ragged at tax time trying to make sense of your paper trail. If you abhor record keeping, look for a bookkeeper rather than a CPA, whose advice may run from $40 to $200 an hour. Bookkeepers start as low as $10 an hour. To find the names of freelance bookkeepers, accountants, typists, and word processors who offer affordable rates, monitor the classified sections of community newspapers—*The Northwest Current, City Paper, Washington Tribune,* and others. (Ask for references and resumes; qualified people never balk at that request.)

You might also try the student route if your needs are simple. At the Small Business Development Center, according to a counselor there, they'll set you up with a motivated accounting or bookkeeping student who might trade time (or a small fee) for the experience of helping a self-employed writer organize tax records. Also, try professors in business departments or the career development centers of nearby colleges for names of bright students preparing for the CPA exam.

One reason why you might spend the extra money to hire a CPA is that they also act as financial advisors for well-off writers. And they are more likely to be knowledgeable about the latest tax law. It could cost a freelance writer from $400 to $500 a year to pay a CPA to update business records and handle taxes. Sometimes you can cut costs by hiring an accountant to review completed tax forms. Some writers prefer to have an attorney handle their tax matters.

## Legal Aid

These are the litigious times that try journalists' souls. Problems applicable to writers include negotiating contracts, reviewing employment and book contracts, copyright law, libel questions, and fee disputes. Fees in town run from virtually nothing for lawyers willing to donate their work, to as high as $250 an hour, according to Alice Bodley, director of the Lawyer Referral and Information Service of the D.C. Bar. Call for a free pamphlet on how to hire a lawyer. (The numbers of the five local bar associations in the metropolitan area are listed in the SBA directory and in the telephone directory.) Each bar association offers a referral service that tries to match a lawyer's specialty with a client's particular problem.

If the thought of large legal bills has you tearing out your hair, there is an alternative. You might not have to pay all at once. Many lawyers will work out an extended payment plan with credit terms as liberal as The Hecht Company and Woodward & Lothrop. Other attorneys discount legal services. It's a competitive market and there are as many job-seeking lawyers out there as there are assignment-seeking writers.

Don't begrudge the profession's high rates when you sorely need advice. Lawyers who charge $150 an hour may be worth their weight in pinstripes. You may ask your friend, the lawyer with a general practice, to write up an employment contract, but, says the D.C. Bar's Bodley, "for copyright and royalty questions it's best to get help from attorneys with relevant expertise."

The firm of Goldfarb, Singer and Austern, headed by attorney-writer Ronald L. Goldfarb, has designed a legal services program for WIW members. For an annual administrative charge, WIW members and their families get a free half-hour consultation on writing-related and other problems, and then one-third off the firm's regular hourly rates. Ronald Schechter of the firm says the hourly rates are "generally not negotiable, but some matters can be arranged on a contingency fee basis." Schechter offers this advice: "Memorialize all verbal agreements. Get everything in writing. *Everything.*"

One place to go for free legal services if you have an art-related problem is the Lawyers Committee for the Arts, also known as Volunteer Lawyers for the Arts, with offices in Georgetown. To be eligible, your previous year's earnings must not have exceeded $7,500. Joshua J. Kaufman, founding director of LCA, says the organization also provides a legal referral service to members of the arts community, houses an art and entertainment law library, and offers lectures and workshops. Kaufman is managing partner of Lowe, Bressler and Kaufman, which specializes in arts (including literary) and entertainment law. The D.C. Commission on the Arts and Humanities is setting up a pro bono legal aid program in conjunction with local law schools. The program will be headed by a fulltime staff lawyer, and is intended to "make legal expertise available to the arts," says Rickie Orchin, special projects coordinator for the commission.

If you need help getting access to public documents, contact the Freedom of Information Center in the offices of the Reporters' Committee for Freedom of the Press (800 18th Street, NW). Reporters' Committee lawyers answer questions about libel and free press issues without charge. A 24-hour hotline (202/466-6312) has been established to advise journalists on pressing First Amendment issues.

To avert legal wrangles, become familiar with newly revised copyright laws. You may pick up a copy at the U.S. Copyright Office in the Madison Building of the Library of Congress, or call their 24-hour hotline (202/287-9100) to record your order for the *General Guide to the Copyright Act of 1976.*

## Health Insurance

The hidden costs of the freelance life become all too apparent when you begin to shop around for health insurance. It's essential to buy adequate coverage, as those caught without it when disaster strikes know too well. Yet, writes Marietta Whittlesey in *Freelance Forever: Successful Self-Employment* (New York: Avon Books, 1982), health insurance "is one of the prime areas of discrimination against self-employed workers." If you're trying to figure out how to buy insurance, you've already discovered it costs much more to buy an individual policy. Moreover, such policies usually cover less than those of a group plan.

Fortunately, choices exist, and it's wise to shop around. Lately, insurance prices have been on the rise, some premiums even doubling within a year. Even the oppressed self-employed may band together and share an insurance plan at group prices. That's what more than 25,000 individuals across the country did after joining the Small Business Services Bureau. (The sole criterion for membership is working for yourself.) The $50-a-year annual membership brings with it access to an extended benefit package with Blue Cross/Blue Shield of Washington. SBSB's downtown office is only an answering service, but details from their Worcester, Massachusetts offices are available toll free, at 800/225-7312.

Locally, members of Washington Independent Writers are eligible for either of two plans. One is the George Washington University Health Plan, a health maintenance organization (1229 25th Street, NW). For a fixed quarterly payment, subscribers of this plan are offered full medical coverage—a range of preventive services, as well as physician and hospital care. (Prepaid individual coverage is also available from the area's two largest

HMOs—the 115,000-member Group Health Association and the Kaiser-Georgetown Community Health Plan, with 82,000 members.)

Alternatively, WIW members have access to a Blue Cross/Blue Shield major medical plan for individuals, administered by the Cultural Alliance of Greater Washington. They also automatically receive a life insurance policy with this plan.

If you pay the topscale fee to join the Cultural Alliance on your own—$55 as opposed to $35—you are eligible to sign up for life insurance coverage from American Banker's Life at group rates, along with its health insurance plan. Still another organization that gives its members access to a Blue Cross/Blue Shield major medical plan for individuals is the Association of Part-Time Professionals—Washington area chapter—in McLean, Virginia. Membership costs $30 a year.

Temporary policies are a great short-term bargain for the premium poor or for freelance writers between jobs. They are available for periods of three or six months or one year. Usually they are nonrenewable with a limit on the number of policies an individual can buy. And some companies offer comprehensive coverage at surprisingly low rates.

If you'd like to become more familiar with health insurance terms, write for the free booklet, "What You Should Know About Health Insurance," from the Health Insurance Association of America, 1850 K Street, NW, Washington, DC 20006.

## Going For a Grant

Who gets grant money? Colleges, foundations, Nobel scientists—and even Washington writers. The simple truth is that those who receive the money are those (with talent) who apply for it. Much more is available than you might imagine.

Most counties in the Washington metropolitan area sponsor arts councils to encourage the promotion of local talent. The Montgomery County Arts Council, for instance, serves as an information center and advocate for the arts. It has a grants library as well. Check with your county government office to find out what facilities, programs, and funds are available to you in your community.

The purses get fatter on the state level. Get in touch with the

Virginia Arts Council in Richmond, the Maryland Arts Council in Baltimore, and the D.C. Commission on the Arts and Humanities to learn about current prizes and awards, deadlines for submissions, and eligibility requirements. Although each operates differently, all have money to give away.

The independent federal grant-making agencies—the National Endowment for the Arts and the National Endowment for the Humanities—are accessible to Washington's creative writers, but, as one NEA administrator points out, "People have an impressive track record before they come to us."

Make tracks of your own in hunting down sources of funds. Visit the Foundation Center (1001 Connecticut Avenue, NW) and browse through the reference library. Also contact the English departments of local universities, which serve as clearinghouses of sorts for information on prizes and awards. Don't overlook the Washington Independent Writers *Newsletter,* the current edition of *Literary Market Place,* and the research library at The Writer's Center in Bethesda. Each is a valuable resource for Washington writers who want to keep informed on literary fellowships, grants, contests, markets, and other ways of breaking even in the writing profession.

## Searching for Work Space

Some writers can't work at home. The isolation may be intolerable, the distractions continuous, or perhaps it's just the sense that if you don't leave your living quarters, you're not really working. Work space in Washington, especially in prime areas, may cost you as much as $24 a square foot, or anywhere from $500 to more than $1,500 a month. Add to that the cost of furnishings and secretarial services.

Be persistent; there are other options. Decide whether you must have access to public transportation, or whether a suburban location would suit you. Knock on the office doors of friends, law firms, even association headquarters, to ask about office space to lease. Go to your neighborhood haunt to scour bulletin boards for notices. Call a university housing office and see what arrangements the academic community may offer.

One association executive who recently hunted down choice office property for her organization says: "Call any agent. They tend to promote the properties they represent, but will give you a sense of what's out there." Check the Yellow Pages for the names of agencies that cater to the smaller renter.

Take out an ad in the community papers. Perhaps you will be the answer to an elderly couple's wish to turn an empty Georgetown parlor into a writer's office during the day. A more direct route is to advertise in the Association of Part-Time Professionals' newsletter or place a classified ad with WIW. Try canvassing local businesses that have cut back on staff to see if one might accommodate an independent writer's part-time presence at a negotiable fee. (Try real estate firms.) Also, see whether you can sublease a space through another tenant.

But if you want it all—semi-private or fulltime office space at a downtown address, telephone answering service, mail drop, editorial and secretarial services—consider The WorkPlace Inc. Catering to freelance professionals in a large office sectioned off into work spaces by flexible partitions, the WorkPlace (1302 18th Street, NW, near the Dupont Circle Metro) is set up to suit individual needs. Short- and long-term contracts may be made for the services and spaces you choose. Charges run from $100 to $500 per month.

## Finding the Basics

"I love rush jobs" says the typist's ad running in one of Washington's community newspapers. Similar notices appear constantly in other papers or are posted on the bulletin boards of English departments, laundromats, and eateries around town. Now is the time to clip notices and compile a list of names and numbers, rather than waiting until your next deadline.

Beware: people who say they do rush jobs sometimes charge excessive rates. A telephone survey of service establishments and independents who advertise their speedy turnaround showed clearly that someone wanting a manuscript typed immediately might be disappointed. For typing or large copying jobs, three days' notice is often required. Ask what "rush job" means.

The cheapest way to get copies is to do them yourself. Self-service places charge as little as four cents a page; otherwise you'll pay an average of a dime apiece.

Here's how to build up your files:

**Word processing.** The Writer's Center rents time on word processors to its members. Workshops are offered at beginning, intermediate, and advanced levels of expertise, at $40 for the four-hour workshop and two hours of practice. Rates at the center—$3.25 an hour, $3 each for 20 hours, and $2.75 each for 50 hours—are the cheapest in town, especially compared to the rates charged by commercial facilities downtown, which typically rent machines during business hours on weekdays for $12, less during evenings and weekends. Besides word processing, The Writer's Center has typesetting, darkroom, and copying services at low rates.

Professional word processors charge widely varying rates—from $7 an hour to more than $20 an hour charged by one editorial service that proofreads all copy.

**Phone Answering.** If you leave your desk and no one is there to take messages, that's not good for business. For this reason many writers buy answering machines, or, if more clicks than messages are recorded, sign up for phone services.

Now might be the time to buy if you've put off purchasing a telephone-answering machine. Machines with remote capability—enabling you to call in for messages from any phone—that until recently cost more than $200 can be found now for as little as $100. Of course, look for advertised discounts in the competitive market.

There's an incredible array of services offered and prices charged for answering services. Don't settle for the first company that quotes you its high and low rates for personalized lines to strictly message-taking services. It is unusual to be charged more than $50 a month to have a live voice answer your phone, but if you dig through the Yellow Pages and the classifieds, you may find someone charging as little as $10 a month to answer during business hours. Ask if you can join with a friend or two on one line to keep costs down. You might also consider signing up with the phone company for call forwarding. After all, a writer must figure out some way to get messages, even if it's only phone privileges at a local tavern.

**Mail forwarding.** A new kind of business has sprung up recently in Washington. For a small monthly fee companies provide a District of Columbia address. The address is really a cubicle where your mail is sorted and then forwarded or picked up by you. Almost all the firms provide telephone answering services, billed either in combination with a private post office box or separately. The cheapest mail drop is still a U.S. post office box, but the waiting list is long at most locations.

**Posting with haste.** Even though the U.S. Postal Service is open 24 hours at National Airport and until midnight at the main office at North Capitol Street and Massachusetts Avenue, Express Mail is the only sure bet for a desperate writer. A manuscript due tomorrow in a distant city must be dropped off at an Express Mail post office by 5 p.m. for guaranteed next-day delivery at 3 p.m. You won't save much money by using a private package courier, but you may save time.

**And more . . .** If your subjects and verbs disagree, correct word usage is a not-so-long-distance call away—to Frostburg, Maryland. Faculty members of the Frostburg State College English Department answer the "Grammarphone" weekday mornings from ten to noon. The number is 301/689-4327, another treasured resource for your Rolodex or well-worn black book.

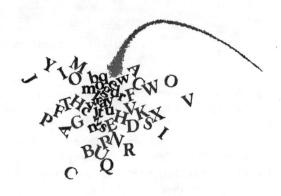

# Book Publishers

Lois Berkowitz

There is a small but growing book publishing industry in Washington. Books of all sorts are being acquired, edited, produced, and marketed here. While New York remains the publishing center of the nation and many Washington books are political, reflecting the city's power base, the field is still livelier than even many writers realize.

Of some two dozen publishing houses now operating in and about Washington, most publish from two to 20 books a year; only one, Reston Publishing, lists 200 titles. Few local houses are interested in fiction and many produce only "academic" titles; that is, books of interest to a specific group of professionals in a specific area of expertise. (Academic books are generally sold by direct mail or through schools.) However, there is a market for nonfiction trade books. (Trade books are those sold through

---

*Former WIW Board member Lois Berkowitz has been a freelance writer for six years. She has written numerous feature articles, mainly on topics of local interest. She also writes and edits newsletters, does PR, copywriting, and other editorial projects.*

bookstores.) And Washington's trade market seems to be growing in new and exciting directions.

Washington also has many publishers who don't fit easily into the "academic" or "trade" categories. The whole spectrum is represented among the members of The Washington Book Publishers, an informal association that has about 200 members. What is the range of book publishers in the Washington area? Of the academics, the Reston Publishing Company is by far the biggest, publishing postsecondary textbooks on agriculture, real estate, business, nursing and paramedical topics, and more. Reston also produces some trade books and computer software. A Prentice-Hall subsidiary, it uses the parent company for warehousing and billing. A smaller division of Prentice-Hall, the Robert J. Brady Company, also publishes textbooks in nursing and allied health fields, and books for emergency medical technicians and firefighters.

Another good-sized (40 to 50 books a year) academic publisher is the Hemisphere Publishing Corporation, which issues texts in the areas of engineering, toxicology, and nursing. While Hemisphere maintains a large office nearby in Bowie, Maryland, its acquisitions department is in New York.

Business, minerals, and energy are the primary topics of specialized books published here by McGraw-Hill (a division of the McGraw-Hill Publications Company, not the McGraw-Hill Book Company). According to Loren Hickman, McGraw-Hill Publications' Editor-in-Chief, "We're here because the government is a great fount of information." This division has a built-in direct-mail market—those who subscribe to its many business periodicals. Also heavily academic are the University Press of America, with a wide range of college and graduate level textbooks; Public Affairs Press, which publishes texts in social sciences, public affairs, political science, and economics; and the Bureau of National Affairs, a private company that publishes in the fields of labor relations, law, energy, environment, and taxes, mainly for the benefit of clients who subscribe to its other services.

Another group of local publishers, all smaller than the ones mentioned so far (25 books a year or fewer), may be categorized as part academic, part trade, but highly specialized in subject area. Their books serve the research and academic communities, professionals and other interested people, and they are distributed both through academic and trade outlets. For example, Naval Institute Press in Annapolis, which publishes textbooks on marine navigation, also puts out general interest books about naval history, plus encyclopedias, calendars, and other items pertaining to maritime subjects. Communications Press produces texts and trade books on communications, science, technology, and public affairs. The Preservation Press, part of the National Trust for Historic Preservation, focuses on preservation, restoration, planning, and architectural history; and Computer Science Press specializes in telecommunications, electrical engineering, and computer science. All these publishers, even the tiniest, such as Denlinger's (dogs), Tarharka in Annapolis (African and Afro-American subjects), and Gryphon House (mainly a distributor, but also a publisher of children's activity books), and others that come and go, are interested in talking to authors who write in their specific areas.

Even more specialized are the publishers that produce books on local subjects. These are trade book publishers, but their subject matter is so localized that their products can be sold only in the immediate area. They tend to know the local market very well and are on good terms with local bookstore owners, so they are often successful. Andrea Lubershane and Erik Kanin, who together comprise Andrik Associates, report that they have sold more than 20,000 copies of some books—fine sales figures in any market. Cornell Maritime Press does nicely with items about the Chesapeake Bay, Maryland Historic Press with books about Maryland, and Potomac Books with local guides.

Recent developments indicate that Washington may be on its way to cornering a share of the trade book market. New York houses have begun to base editors here. For example, Harcourt Brace Jovanovich, which in the past concerned itself only with business magazine publishing in Washington, recently added trade book editor, Marie Arana-Ward, to its Washington office. In her words, "Where there is good journalism, there is good potential for books." Harcourt Brace says it is looking for fiction and nonfiction of all kinds.

In addition, New Republic Books has been taken over by Holt, Rinehart & Winston, and New Republic's Washington Editor, Marc Granetz, is now in the business of acquiring titles under the New Republic imprint and the Holt name. Granetz says, "There are lots of people here who have written with an academic approach. I'd like to take their work and give it a more popular approach . . . turn it into a serious trade book."

And as New York is coming to Washington, Washington is going to New York in the person of Joel Makower, president of Tilden Press Inc., which is probably the first Washington publisher to get into the business of book packaging. Besides putting out its own books on consumer and how-to topics, Tilden has packaged books for Penguin, Doubleday, Simon & Schuster, and other New York publishers. In effect, Tilden acts as agent for the author and editor and production department for the publisher—an interesting new approach.

It is unclear what effect the coming of New York companies will have on the local trade book market, but right now Washington has several small trade book publishers (in addition to the ones that deal with purely local topics). Largest and best known of these is Acropolis Books, which started in 1960 as an offshoot of a printing firm, Colortone Press. Acropolis now publishes 25 to 40 books a year, mostly self-help and how-to volumes. Smaller but up-and-coming are Tilden; Calvin Kytle's Seven Locks Press, which has done books on Gandhi, opinion polls, political and local subjects; Evelyn Metzger's EPM Publications, which features travel books, local guides, and craft books; and Mark Esterman's Great Ocean Publishers, which has published an eclectic mix of memoirs, books on child development, and various other subjects. The output of each of these small operations is fewer than ten books a year.

No survey of the Washington publishing scene would be complete without mention of university presses. These often spring from the output of one college or department at a university. Such is the case at Georgetown, whose press began in the language and linguistics area. Georgetown University Press is now expanding into the rather large and amorphous area of ethics, with an output of eight to ten books a year. Howard University Press, about the same size, concerns itself with subjects relating to minorities and the Third World. Johns Hopkins University Press in Baltimore, a larger (100 books a year) and less specialized operation, is best known for its books on literature, political science, economics, and medicine. Gallaudet

College Press was founded in 1980 and publishes six to eight books a year, most of them for professionals and teachers in the field of hearing impairment.

Mention should also be made of local "literary presses." (These are often called "small presses," but so many of Washington's publishers are small that these deserve a different designation.) Although poets and short story writers rarely expect (or receive) great monetary rewards from their work, they *do* want to see it published, and literary presses are where they go. Best known and oldest of the current literary crop is Merrill Leffler's Dryad Press, which publishes a variety of fine works, usually with a first printing of 600 to 2,500 copies. How well the books do often depends on how many readings an author can line up. Two other well-known local literary presses are Doug Messerli's Sun and Moon Press and the Washington Writers' Publishing House, a writers' cooperative.

Another large part of Washington's publishing scene may be called, for want of a better word, "association" publishing. This is a very general category in which to lump books put out by Washington's ever-growing numbers of nonprofit trade associations, professional groups, government agencies, think tanks, and the like. Most association publications are written by staff members rather than by independent writers. If you are a former staff member, or if you have expertise in a specialized area and if you are well-known for your expertise, you may be able to find work in association publishing.

Your chances are slightly better for contracting to write a book or section of a book for a few other organizations in town that fall into a separate category. These include *National Geographic, Congressional Quarterly,* the Smithsonian Institution, and Time-Life Books. The difference here is that *they,* not you, originate the idea for a book and they generally determine its structure, contents, and style. You contract with them on a work-for-hire basis and do not own the rights to the book or receive royalties. Like trade associations, these organizations will turn to their staff members first, but if nobody with the proper expertise is available, they will look to independent writers.

Once you are familiar with the gamut of Washington publishers, you may wish to ask why a writer should, or shouldn't, use a local publisher. On the "should" side of this question is friendly support and ease of communication. At a small local house you can establish a comfortable relationship with your editor/publisher and have more influence on publishing decisions. You don't necessarily have to work through an agent to submit a manuscript or proposal here, not even to Harcourt Brace or Holt. If your book is academic and your aim in writing it is not mass circulation, academic publishers here are fine. If your subject is highly specialized, a local publisher who knows that subject thoroughly may do as good a job for you as a larger publisher. And certainly, if your subject is local, there is no point in trying to sell your book to a publisher outside this area.

In addition, an outfit that publishes only ten books a year will work hard to sell those ten, whereas a publisher of 500 books a year may only concentrate on the "blockbusters." Smaller publishers can and do maintain bigger backlists, pushing your book year after year, so even if you don't make money "up front," you might make some in the long run. One other argument in favor of a local publisher—credentials. If you are totally unknown, it is often easier to place your book with a local house. If the book sells well, you will have acquired a credential that will help you place your second book, either here or in New York.

The strongest argument against approaching a local publisher boils down to money. Most local publishers are too small to give sizeable advances and many don't even offer them. Some offer good royalty percentages, but your book has to sell long and well for that to make a difference. Most New York publishers use a standard contract, while local houses usually work on a case-by-case basis, which may or may not be to your advantage. If your object is to get your book into the big book store chains, you'll do better with New York publishers because they have larger sales and distribution networks. They also have more advertising dollars to spend. (The trick, of course, is convincing them to spend those dollars on you.)

Before you try to sell your book, interview both local and New York publishers. Don't be embarrassed to ask questions. Here are some to keep in mind: What is the audience for your book? Does the publishing house have access to the market you want to reach? How does it reach that market? How well do its books sell? Does it sell books in your subject area? How many? Is the company well known in your subject area? Does the publisher

offer standard hardback and paperback royalties? If not, what
kinds of royalties *are* offered? Who will own what percentage
of the subsidiary rights? What other authors does the house
publish? How long is the publisher willing to keep your book
"alive?"

The more informed you are, the better off you will be in dealing with any publisher, local or otherwise. To become better informed you may want to use the services of local publications
consultants. For a fee, these people will help you structure your
book, advise on graphics, suggest marketing strategies, and
make the whole publishing process clearer. They will also help
with self-publishing ventures. Local consultants include Al
Staats & Associates, Andromeda Associates, Tilden Press, Great
Ocean Publishers, and Samuel Blate Associates.

You may also wish to look for a literary agent, remembering
that it's often as hard to be signed by a good agent as by a good
publisher. A comprehensive list of agents—mainly New York-
based—may be obtained from the Society of Authors Representatives, P.O. Box 650, Old Chelsea Station, New York, NY 10113.

A small number of agents work out of Washington. Some are
more active and accessible than others, but all report that they're
doing well. They experience no problem at being a distance from
New York. Rafe Sagalyn (Raphael Sagalyn Inc., 2813 Bellevue
Terrace, NW, Washington, DC 20007; 202/337-9660) says, "All
my business is done by phone so it doesn't matter that I'm not
in New York." Audrey Adler Wolf (1000 Potomac Street, NW,
Suite 105, Washington, DC 20007; 202/333-2702) travels to New
York frequently but feels that the miles are no difficulty. "What
I need and want is good clients," she says. "Publishers are
always available and I can get to them."

Agent Ann Buchwald (4327 Hawthorne Street, NW, Washington, DC 20016; 202/362-2912) handles adult fiction and nonfiction. She notes, "Washington agents came into being because
it is harder for the writer of a first book to get a New York agent
than a publisher."

Besides those mentioned above, other local agents include:
Agronsky & Kraft, 2828 Connecticut Avenue, NW, Washington,
DC 20008; 202/332-2626
BSW Literary Agency Inc., 3255 N Street, NW, Washington,
DC 20007; 202/342-0142

Larry Kaltman, 1301 South Scott Street, Arlington, VA 22204; 703/920-3771

Literary Agency of Washington, 2025 I Street, NW, Washington, DC 20037; 202/466-7399

Leona Schecter, 3748 Huntington Street, NW, Washington, DC 20015; 202/362-9040

Roberta E. Sodsisky, Sodsisky & Sons, 5914 Greentree Road, Bethesda, MD 20817; 301/897-8444

Some lawyers today are also taking on the agent's role. Prominent among these is local attorney Ronald Goldfarb (Goldfarb, Singer and Austern, 918 16th Street, NW, Washington, DC 20006; 202/466-3030). Says Goldfarb of his firm, "We do everything agents do, but we don't consider ourselves agents because we provide legal services as well."

With a growing number of publishing houses and at least a handful of agents, Washington is becoming better and better equipped to serve the needs of local book writers. You may say without hesitation that book publishing is alive and well on the Potomac. While not the hub of the publishing world, Washington is certainly a respectable spoke of the industry's wheel.

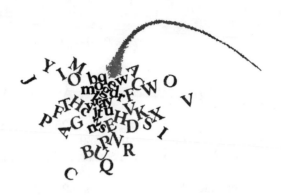

# Publications

## Richard Peabody

The nation's capital is home to specialized interests and specialized magazines. The flood of information generated by the federal government alone in this area has necessitated the birth of a gargantuan print industry unlike that found anywhere else in the country.

Magazines run the gamut from primarily staff-written publications like *U.S. News & World Report* and *Changing Times*, neither of which uses much freelance material, to *American Film* and *The American Scholar*, which rely extensively on the work freelance writers provide. In fact there are so many outlets that the energetic freelance writer is torn between submitting material to prestige journals like *The New Republic* and *The Washington Monthly*, which pay little, or those aimed at a much narrower audience like *SciQuest Magazine* and *Government Executive*, which pay a lot. Despite today's variety, the area was initially slow in attracting magazine publishers of any kind. Both

*Richard Peabody edits* Gargoyle, *a literary magazine. A Washington native, his book of poems is* I'm in Love with the Morton Salt Girl. *He recently edited* D.C. Magazines: A Literary Retrospective *and* Mavericks: Nine Small Publishers.

Baltimore and Charleston, South Carolina, beat Washington to the punch.

The first actual magazine published in Washington was the *National Magazine; or Cabinet of the United States*, which moved here from Richmond, Virginia in 1801. At the time there were only 12 magazines in the entire country.

Before 1900 few magazines were attempted, though notable exceptions include *National Geographic*, founded here in 1888 (and still going strong today); journals founded at Georgetown and Howard Universities in 1882 and 1893, respectively; *Paul Pry*, founded in 1831 by Anne Royall, a gossipy magazine that combined politics with social life and could be considered a forerunner of "The Ear" column; and *The Washingtonian*, which made a five-month go of it in 1897. The turn of the century brought the early forebears of today's *Washingtonian* and *Washington Dossier: Washington Mirror* (1900-1905), *Washington Life* (1903-1906), and other imitators.

## Major Markets

Washington has to be taken seriously as a major freelance market if only for success stories like *Science 83*, *Smithsonian Magazine*, *The New Republic*, *American Film*, *The Washington Monthly*, and *National Geographic*. There may not be as many alternatives here as there are in New York, but the bona fide success of independents outside the sphere of the Big Apple's publishing world is certainly a healthy sign.

Many popular national magazines have Washington bureaus, including *Life*, *Fortune*, *Forbes*, *Time*, *Newsweek*, *Variety*, *Sports Illustrated*, *Ebony*, *Jet*, and *TV Guide*. Some of the larger magazines depend on stringers. Other organizations enjoy Washington headquarters but are published out of town, such as the Natural Resources Defense Council, whose *Amicus Journal* is published in New York, or the American Association of Retired Persons, whose *Modern Maturity* is based in California.

Every magazine has its own favored stable of writers, including freelance writers, but there's no reason that familiarity with a publication's style and format, a bright idea, or good timing won't land an article or review.

Freelance writers should be aware that *National Geographic* is an excellent market (circulation is upwards of ten million), but that thinking up an idea, which isn't in competition with one incredible adventure saga or another, is going to be time-consuming and difficult.

The boom in high-tech and science-oriented magazines and the number of scientific facilities and organizations hereabouts makes *Science 83* a good market to try. It has room for those who want to open communication channels between the often impenetrable jargon of the scientific community and the public.

If you've got inside information on the cinema, *American Film* is the place to try. It draws features from critics and interviewers nationwide.

In the civic arena, *Inquiry* is an influential monthly that combines political emphasis with arts savvy. *The New Republic* is a Washington institution and, being a weekly journal of opinion, burns up a lot of material. *The Washington Monthly* also has a solid reputation and is another likely target.

The Smithsonian Institution publishes two prestigious magazines. *Smithsonian Magazine* welcomes a wide range of material and is a strong market for freelance writers. The Institution's Woodrow Wilson International Center for Scholars produces the *Wilson Quarterly*, a magazine devoted to public affairs, and coverage of the center's activities.

Another good local freelance market is *Regardies*, a magazine on Washington business and real estate, which also looks for articles on labor and financial issues.

*National Wildlife*, published by the National Wildlife Federation, is a slick along the lines of *National Geographic*. Sharing a similar domain are *Living Wilderness*, a bimonthly produced by the Wilderness Society, and *International Wildlife*.

Two magazines that cover the local scene are *The Washingtonian* and its younger competitor, *Washington Dossier*. Both focus on events and personalities around town. *Washingtonian* is perhaps the largest magazine user of freelance material in the area. Like other city magazines, this financially successful publication employs freelance writers for many of its service pieces as well as for many of its major articles.

Those of a literary bent may turn to *The American Scholar*. Critical entries and original works are welcomed, though their stress is heavily academic. While *The Washington Post* generally goes for established names when it comes to the book reviews in its Sunday "Book World," there is always the possibility that a freelance writer's aptitude for a particular subject, or intimacy with an individual author's work, will fit their bill.

*Washington Journalism Review* draws its writers from journalism, politics, and the media. Familiarity might garner an acceptance. But remember that since Watergate the streets of Washington are paved with journalists. *National Journal,* a respected weekly on government policy and politics, occasionally uses freelance writers for its in-depth stories.

*Country Magazine,* in Alexandria, is an attractive newcomer that found its niche with the back-to-nature crowd. While much of the work it publishes is staff-written, or farmed out to many associate editors, it appears genuinely open to fresh ideas. *Maryland Magazine* and *Chesapeake Bay Magazine* cater to a similar audience. Articles on a particular place, or the right human interest feature, might bring a positive response.

The Sunday *Washington Post Magazine* reaches an enormous audience. Lately the magazine has stressed thematic issues which leave less opportunity for outsiders. These things run in cycles.

The United States Information Agency publishes several magazines including *Dialogue: Arts in America, America Illustrated, Topic,* and *Problems of Communism,* for consumption overseas. USIA normally assigns freelance work.

## Specialty Magazines

Specialty magazines range from *Middle East Economic Digest* and *Ob Gyn News* to *Chemical and Radiation Waste Litigation Reporter, The Psychic Observer,* and *Rural Electrification Magazine.* You name it, and there's a good possibility it exists someplace nearby. The American Police Academy's *Bounty Hunter International* is a perfect example. This publication is dedicated to finding missing persons; it features exposes, personal narratives, and interviews with the missing and those who find them.

Investigative reporters might want to look into *Counter Spy* or *Victimology: An International Journal,* two magazines that specialize in blowing the lids off injustice.

There aren't many local music magazines (odd for a town that claims Duke Ellington as a native son). One that's been quite steady is *Jazz Times*, which is open to reviews and interviews. The music tabloid, *Unicorn Times*, is more rock-oriented. Other specialized music magazines have come and gone as quickly as mayflies.

Those who write for the *Science 83* market might want to get acquainted with *The Futurist*, produced in Bethesda by the World Future Society. Contributors aren't paid, but the magazine reaches a wide audience and is geared more to hard facts and educated speculation than a glamor market like *Omni*.

*New Art Examiner* is a Chicago-based arts tabloid that features correspondents from many U.S. cities. They seem very receptive to local talent and have an established base in the area.

*off our backs* is one of the oldest feminist voices in the country, while *The Washington Blade* and *Out* reflect Washington's gay community.

While *American Film* is intended for the cinemaphile with stress on stars and lots of splashy color, a new quarterly printed in Annapolis, *In Motion*, covers the more technical aspects of film and video production.

Heldref Foundation publishes 39 different magazines from its Albemarle Street headquarters. Each caters to a separate freelance market. Titles include *The Journal of Arts Management and Law, Journal of Popular Film & Television, Design for Arts in Education, American Record Guide, Journal of African Studies,* and *Germanic Review*. Any of these could give a freelance writer experience, though little or no money.

Two local children's magazines are *World*, published by the National Geographic Society, and *Ranger Rick's Nature Magazine*, put out by the National Wildlife Federation. They're meant for kids from 6 to 12.

The National Zoo publishes several magazines, one of which, *Zoogoer*, takes about 75 percent of its material from freelance writers. Equine lovers might fare well at *Horsemen's Journal*.

The Aircraft Owners and Pilots Association in Bethesda produces *The AOPA Pilot*, which covers everything from maintenance tips to the legal aspects of owning and operating aircraft. *Vertiflite* is a similar magazine designed for the helicopter set. *Parachutist*, on the other hand, is a phenomenally successful monthly dedicated to the disciples of that sport.

Washington is also home to the military's many journals—
*Air Force Magazine, Army Magazine, Marine Corps Gazette,
Leatherneck, U.S. Naval Institute Proceedings, Soldier's
Magazine, Shipmate, Ladycom Magazine,* and *The Times
Magazine* supplement to *Army Times, Navy Times,* and *Air
Force Times.*

## Trade Markets

Every trade association and institute seems to have a magazine,
newsletter, or bulletin of its very own. These are often PR sheets,
or in-house organs for members of the particular organization.
Those that do consider unsolicited submissions require a degree
of expertise or at least familiarity with the business lacking in
the average freelance writer. Before contributing something to
a trade publication, writers would be well advised to be sure of
their material, and aware of the marketplace.

Obviously, magazines like *Air Line Pilot, Professional Pilot
Magazine, The Typographer, Security Management, Symphony
Magazine, The Chemist, Parking,* or *Cemetery Management,* are
going to be hard for the uninitiated to crack.

Education magazines are difficult markets—*Education USA,
American Teacher, American Educator,* and *Graduate Woman*
use next to no freelance material.

*Listen Magazine,* a drug education publication for young
adults, uses 50 percent freelance material. It leans toward nar-
rative experience and hard information on successful drug reform
activities. *Your Life and Health* is a more accessible freelance
market, featuring general health articles written in language
anyone can understand.

Other open markets include *Public Citizen Magazine,* which
is published by a consumer group founded by Ralph Nader and
deals with consumer issues; *Historic Preservation,* which deals
with specific sites and neighborhood planning; *Mass Transit,*
which sends freelance writers on assignment; and *Foreign Policy
Magazine,* which, as the name implies, looks for coverage of U.S.
foreign policy issues.

This list by no means exhausts every potential publisher. If
you possess expertise in a specific trade, it would be to your
advantage to scour the phone book and various directories to
locate a market suited to your talent.

# Names and Addresses

Publications that are referred to here but not presently listed in local directories include:

*Abbey,* 5011-2 Green Mountain Circle, Columbia, MD 21044

*Afro-Hispanic Review,* 3306 Ross Place, NW, Washington, DC 20008

*Alph Null,* 17 Logan Circle, NW, Washington, DC 20005

*Bogg,* 422 North Cleveland Street, Arlington, VA 22201

*Calvert Review,* c/o Maryland Media Inc., University of Maryland, College Park, MD 20740

*Chimaera,* 1309 Duke Street, Alexandria, VA 22314

*City Paper,* 919 6th Street, NW, Washington, DC 20001

*Columbia Road,* 1637 Harvard Street, NW, Washington, DC 20009

*Columbia Road Review,* P.O. Box 19332, Washington, DC 20036

*Counterspy,* 647 Benjamin Franklin Station, Washington, DC 20044

*DEROS,* 6009 Edgewood Lane, Alexandria, VA 22310

*Federal Poet,* 5321 Willard Avenue, Chevy Chase, MD 20015

*Gargoyle,* P.O. Box 3567, Washington, DC 20007

*GW Review,* Marvin Center Box 20, George Washington University, 800 21st Street, NW, Washington, DC 20052

*In Motion,* 301 4th Street, Annapolis, MD 21403

*Maryland Magazine,* 2525 Riva Road, Annapolis, MD 21401

*Nethula Journal,* P.O. Box 50368, Washington, DC 20004

*Omowee Review,* Room 110, The Blackburn Center, Howard University, Washington, DC 20059

*Parachutist,* 1440 Duke Street, Alexandria, VA 22314

*Parking,* 1101 17th Street, NW, Washington, DC 20036

*Phoebe,* 4400 University Drive, Fairfax, VA 22205

*Poet Lore,* 4000 Albemarle Street, NW, Suite 504, Washington, DC 20016

*Sibyl-Child,* Box 1773, Hyattsville, MD 20788

*Sun & Moon,* 4330 Hartwick Road, No. 418, College Park, MD 20740

*Three Sisters,* Box 969, Georgetown University, Washington, DC 20057

*Thrust,* 8217 Langport Terrace, Gaithersburg, MD 20877

*Verbena,* 1715 Connecticut Avenue, NW, Washington, DC 20009

*Visions,* 5620 South 7th Place, Arlington, VA 22204

*Washington Book Review,* 4577 MacArthur Boulevard, NW, Washington, DC 20007

# Literary Markets

Poets and fiction writers have a variety of outlets from which to choose. *The American Scholar, The New Republic, The Washingtonian, Washington Dossier,* or *Science 83,* already mentioned as nonfiction markets, also publish creative work. Alternative papers such as *City Paper, The Hill Rag,* and *Columbia Road* occasionally publish poetry. Literary magazines boomed here in the 30s and again in the 60s; today we are blessed with all sorts of underground, mid-range, and established journals or reviews. These magazines by their very nature generally last for several issues and then fade quietly from the scene. Readerships range anywhere from the editor's friends and relations to upwards of 2,000 devotees. Some are strictly regional in nature, others full-blown on the international circuit. They don't necessarily pay but usually give their contributors copies of the issue in which the work appears, along with valuable exposure.

Few literary magazines have lasted longer than three years in this town, and of those still publishing that have lasted longer, *Black Box Magazine* stands in a class by itself. One of the earliest cassette poetry magazines in the country, *Black Box Magazine* has been coming out since 1972. It pays modestly for material it accepts. Submissions must be on tape.

A few tabloid arts magazines run everything from interviews to graphics, poems, fiction, and reviews. The *Washington Review* and *Black Arts Review* fill this bill.

Two quarterly magazines which run only book reviews and interviews are the *Washington Book Review* and *Columbia Road Review.* They offer alternatives to the mass market emphasis of *The Washington Post*'s "Book World" and help disseminate information to the booming local literary scene.

Several universities have literary magazines that welcome off-campus submissions and consistently run work from all over the country—*Three Sisters* at Georgetown, the *G.W. Review* at George Washington, *Calvert Review* at the University of Maryland, *Omowee Journal* at Howard, and *Phoebe* at George Mason.

Two magazines have recently been resuscitated—the eight-year-old feminist arts magazine *Sibyl-Child,* and *Chimaera,* a literary magazine now based in Alexandria.

The established literary magazines vary greatly in format and direction—*Verbena: Bilingual Review of the Arts*, appears in both Spanish and English; *Nethula Journal* emphasizes black writers and artists; *Sun and Moon: A Journal of Literature and Art* tips its hat toward the avant-garde, and may or may not be entering publishing limbo; *Thrust: Science Fiction in Review* serves as a critical watchdog for that field; *Poet Lore* (originally founded in Boston in 1889), published by the Heldref Foundation, features poems and reviews exclusively; *Deros* promotes the literary creations of Vietnam veterans; while *Gargoyle* regularly prints interviews, poetry, fiction, graphics, and reviews.

Other local outlets are *Visions* (poetry only), *Bogg* (a mix of British and U.S. poetry, graphics, fiction, and reviews, unique in this country), the *Federal Poet* (poetry only, published continuously since 1946), and *Abbey* (a literary review from nearby Columbia, Maryland). Recent additions are the still untested *Alph Null* and *Afro-Hispanic Review*.

Washington would be a freelance writer's paradise if so many writers weren't furiously working similar ideas. Because of the area's national and international character, writers whistle-stop here from all over the globe, and the idealistic freelance writer faces stiff competition. But there are certainly enough different magazines to publish an ever-changing array of writers. It's an impressive and unpredictable list.

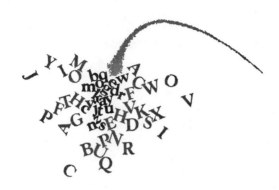

# Bookstores

## Mark Perry

**W**riters are voracious, often compulsive, readers. Most, no doubt the majority, prefer to own the books they use and so consider bookstores as essential as typing paper. Writers haunt bookstores to browse, to supplement library research, to keep apprised of what's being published and of what's selling. For most writers, too, the sight, scent, and feel of both old and new books gives abiding pleasure.

While Washington is without a major all-purpose New York-type book warehouse, there are many excellent independent bookstores in the city that rival the best that New York has to offer. Books are available here in quantity, service is generally good, and such special services as searches outside normal stock selection are offered. The city's community of booksellers is knowledgeable and experienced, and will refer buyers to other sources when they are unable to produce a title.

As a source of used and rare books, Washington ranks high. The number and variety of antiquarian and used bookshops in

*Mark Perry is an independent writer, journalist, and contributor to several national publications who served as book buyer for four years with two of Washington's largest bookstores.*

the metropolitan area has increased dramatically over the last few years. Out-of-print or hard-to-find titles are now easier to locate and a list of 65 bookshops is available from most dealers, titled *A Friend's Guide to the Washington and Baltimore Area Antiquarian and Used Bookshops for the Convenience of Bookscouts and Bibliophiles et al.*

Historically, from Sylvia Beach's Shakespeare & Company in Paris to New York's Strand Bookstore, a symbiotic relationship has existed between the writing community of a given city and the local stores that display its fruits. A writer's bookstore often goes far beyond selling books. It fills special orders, finds that long out-of-print volume without which a writer cannot complete his or her own book, and often promotes the work of local authors.

A chain bookstore is not, by any definition, a writer's bookstore because of the limited number of titles and types of books available. There are three major chain bookstores in the Washington area: **Crown Books** (at 20-plus locations), **B. Dalton Booksellers** (at ten locations), and **Waldenbooks** (at 15 locations). They offer popular hardback and paperback bestsellers and have some hardback classics in all areas.

Below are descriptions of Washington's major independent bookstores. The list is not meant to be complete. For most writers, diligent research is necessary to determine which single store is best for an individual need.

**Backstage Inc.**, 2101 P Street, NW, Washington, DC 20037; 202/775-1488. If you need to buy a book on the performing arts, most good bookstores in Washington will have an arts section. But the only bookstore that specializes in the performing arts is Backstage Inc., which sells plays, books on acting and dance, theatre and movie posters, and stage makeup. The staff is helpful.

**The Book Annex (Record and Tape Ltd.)**, 1239 Wisconsin Avenue, NW, Washington, DC 20007; 202/338-6712; 1340 Connecticut Avenue, NW, Washington, DC 20036; 202/ 785-2662; 106 South Union Street, Alexandria, VA 22314; 703/684-0077.

This is by far the finest book outlet in the city. The Book Annex's Wisconsin Avenue location, in particular, is renowned for its excellent selection of books on politics and history.

What The Book Annex lacks in atmosphere, it more than makes up for in stock selection. Additionally, the sales staff is knowledgeable. The Book Annex has the best book minds in the business; you will not be faced with blank stares. What the store doesn't have, it can usually get, but you are advised to hold the store to a specific time limit in ordering books. The store cannot procure textbooks—except for those that are popular or considered classics—and scientific titles and art titles are only marginally in evidence.

The Book Annex has purchased the old Discount Book Store location on Dupont Circle and turned it into a classy all-purpose store. Its selection in politics, military science, history, and sociology will provide some gems for the writer who spends time getting to know the stock.

**Calliope Bookshop,** 3424 Connecticut Avenue, NW, Washington, DC 20008; 202/364-0111. This is indeed a writer's bookstore. Specializing in literature—fiction, poetry, literary biography, and criticism—it also maintains an impressive selection of backlist titles and small press books.

**Cheshire Cat Children's Book Store,** 5512 Connecticut Avenue, NW, Washington, DC 20015; 202/244-3956. This excellent bookstore with its extensive selection of titles and attractive decor is, perhaps, the most author-oriented store in the city. Writers of children's books are invited to give talks and meet their fans, and local authors are strongly supported.

**Common Concerns,** 1347 Connecticut Avenue, NW, Washington, DC 20036; 202/463-6500. Common Concerns is a bookstore-within-a-bookstore, located in the Kramer Books just below Dupont Circle. It contains one of the best selections of books from the political left and feminist communities available anywhere.

**Francis Scott Key Book Shop,** 28th and O Streets, NW, Washington, DC 20007; 202/337-4144. A find. The best service in town. Everything from popular top-ten bestsellers to paperback classics and children's books are available. The store emphasizes special ordering. Key Book Shop has been around a long time and should be more frequented than it is.

**Globe Book Shops,** 1700 Pennsylvania Avenue, NW, Washington, DC 20006; 202/393-1490;
888 17th Street, NW, Washington, DC 20006; 202/223-6774;
Crystal City Underground, Arlington, VA 22202; 703/521-3443.
Globe's main store at 17th Street and Pennsylvania Avenue, NW is renowned for its selection of foreign language books. But you should take time to review its other sections, particularly fiction and reference books. The main store also features a special order and individual services department—they have good overseas connections, are well-versed in areas not common to other booksellers, and are honest about what they can and cannot do.

**The Kramer Book Stores,** Kramerbooks & Afterwords Cafe, 1517 Connecticut Avenue, NW, Washington, DC 20036; 202/387-1400;
Kramer Books Inc., 1347 Connecticut Avenue, NW, Washington, DC 20036; 202/293-2072;
Kramer Books, Capitol Hill, 336 Pennsylvania Avenue, SE, Washington, DC 20003; 202/547-5990;
Sidney Kramer Books, 1722 H Street, NW, Washington, DC 20006; 202/298-8010.
A journey through all four of the Kramer stores will probably turn up what you want and, if not, the staff can usually provide it in fairly short order. Of the four stores, the Capitol Hill and Kramerbooks & Afterwords locations are the most sparsely stocked, but the Kramerbooks & Afterwords store, with its adjoining cafe, outdistances all in atmosphere.

The 1347 Connecticut Avenue location features remainder books only (books that publishers have discounted due to overstock); it also contains Common Concerns (see above). A quick trip through the store may turn up two or three useful titles, but finding something in the stock that you have been wanting for years is the exception, not the rule.

The 1722 H Street store is probably the most useful for the specialist. Social sciences and economics are emphasized. The special-order services at all of the stores are above average.

**Lammas,** 321 7th Street, SE, Washington, DC 20003; 202/546-7292. Lammas provides both scholarly and popular works on issues important to women, a wide selection of journals and alternative periodicals, small press publications, records, and craft items. Its owner is most willing to special order books not in stock. Lammas functions as an information exchange for Washington's feminist community and sells tickets to local events.

**Maryland Book Exchange,** 4500 College Avenue, College Park, MD 20740; 301/927-2510. Like Reiter's, MBE specializes in hard-to-find textbooks and features 70,000 titles. Looks are deceiving. This is a college bookstore, good for those in Maryland, but for book buyers in Washington or Virginia, Reiter's or a comparable college store should come before a trip to College Park.

**Reiter's Students Book Co.,** 2120 Pennsylvania Avenue, NW, Washington, DC 20037; 202/223-3327. The store specializes in technical, medical, and scientific books. The staff is knowledgeable, but textbooks, the store specialty, are always difficult to obtain. The store will special order a title, but often advises customers to order directly from the publisher. Reiter's is the best bet for obtaining technical books.

**The Smithsonian Bookstore,** (National Museum of American History), 14th Street and Constitution Avenue, NW, Washington, DC 20560; 202/357-1784. This store is apt to be overlooked. It features one of the most complete lines of Americana in the nation, and is hard to beat for American history and political science books.

**Yes! Bookshop,** 1035 31st Street, NW, Washington, DC 20007; 202/338-7874. This store features six spacious rooms of books on alternative psychology, the occult, natural foods, astrology, health, mythology, and both Eastern and Western philosophy.

## Antiquarian and Used Books

**Second Story Books,** 3236 P Street, NW, Washington, DC 20007; 202/244-5550;
2000 P Street, NW, Washington, DC 20036; 202/659-8884;
7730 Old Georgetown Road, Bethesda, MD 20814; 301/656-0170. Second Story Books has the largest collection of used books in the area. The Dupont Circle branch at 2000 P Street, NW, is good, but not as good as that in Georgetown. The Georgetown Second Story Books at 3236 P Street, NW, is by far the best— by virtue of its staff and search capabilities—and is housed in the former Savile Book Shop location, a former Washington literary landmark. It is a big store made up of a warren of small rooms, conducive to browsing for some people, confusing for others. Don't be put off; the buyers are excellent and know the store's stock.

**Booked Up,** 1209 31st Street, NW, Washington, DC 20007; 202/965-3244. This is one of Washington's better known small and excellent rare bookstores. It specializes in rare and scholarly books in all fields with an emphasis on fine first editions, voyages and travels, and natural history.

**Wayward Books,** 1002-B Pennsylvania Avenue, SE, Washington, DC 20003; 202/546-2719. The only antiquarian bookstore on Capitol Hill. Its specialty is modern first editions, but it has a wide general selection and browsers can sit and read undisturbed.

Other sources of used books worth mentioning include: **Book Ends,** 2710 Washington Boulevard, Arlington; 703/524-4976; **The Book Cellar,** 8227 Woodmont Avenue, Bethesda; 301/654-1898; **Bookhouse,** 805 North Emerson Street, Arlington; 703/527-7797; **Estate Book Sales,** 2824 Pennsylvania Avenue, NW; 202/965-4274; **Idle Time Books,** 1723 Columbia Road, NW; 202/232-4774; **Alexander Laubert's Books,** 1073 West Broad Street, Falls Church; 703/533-1699; **Quill and Brush,** 7649 Old

Georgetown Road, Bethesda; 301/951-0919; and **Yesterday's Books**, 4702 Wisconsin Avenue, NW; 202/363-0581 and 3222 M Street, NW; 202/333-8765.

Washington contains more than 200 bookstores, many of which are specialty stores featuring everything from cookbooks (and just cookbooks) to religious books (and just religious books). The key is that the city has a book community, a set of bookstores, and book people who are knowledgeable and helpful.

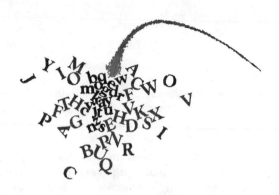

# Writers' Courses

## Kate Weinstein

**A**wise writer once said that "writing is the hardest way of earning a living, with the possible exception of wrestling alligators." Participating in writing courses and workshops is one way to ease the struggle and learn the tools of survival. And while it has also been said that no one can teach another how to write, fortunately for local writers there are a number of schools and groups in the area that aim to prove the old adage false.

No writing course will transform a mediocre writer into a Hemingway or a Fitzgerald. But while talent cannot be taught, it can be developed. Craftsmanship can be polished, honed, and refined; inspiration can be tuned and creativity awakened. For writers of poetry, short stories, novels, plays, and nonfiction, writing courses and workshops offer not formulas and rigid techniques, but mutual support, encouragement, and criticism. A sharing process takes place in which students learn from each other as they try to solve similar problems. The ultimate goal is to train

*Kate Weinstein is a freelance writer and editor whose work has appeared in* The Los Angeles Times. *Her special interests include travel, health, and consumer issues.*

the writer's powers of self-criticism, to open new avenues of self-discovery and perception.

In addition to expanding and improving skills, learning marketing techniques and strategies for advancing in the job market, writers often gain a sense of community and camaraderie by associating with other writers. While some writers appear to thrive in isolation, others find it too lonely an occupation and suffer from a lack of professional identity and outside support. Continuing education in Washington is more than lectures and exercises. Learning, here, is also a social activity. Classrooms are meeting grounds and provide opportunities to make contacts with other writers, editors, artists, future sources of information, and people who hire writers.

The need for continuing education for writers is especially apparent in Washington, where there are so many jobs in researching, writing, and editing. The volume of paperwork that circulates in the District alone is incalculable. Employment opportunities exist in government, corporations, trade associations, nonprofit organizations, journal and book publishers, advertising agencies, consulting firms, museums, and newspapers.

The local demand for talented and qualified individuals is enormous. Writers are needed to produce fund-raising literature, ad copy, press releases, proposals, brochures, newsletters, scripts, articles, and technical materials. Because so much of the writing done here is specialized, tailored to the needs of the communications center of the nation, training opportunities and resources have expanded to meet those needs and specifications.

While the Washington area seems so promising in opportunities for writing and editing careers, it attracts great numbers of highly skilled and exceptional people who want to be a part of the city's corps of professionals. In this extremely competitive job market, specialized training is no longer a luxury, but a necessity. For both staff and freelance writers, the more versatile they are, the greater their value as employees. In times of cutbacks and budget restrictions, writers with additional expertise in areas such as graphics and management will have the inside track.

Following is a sampling of Washington area schools and organizations that offer continuing education to writers. Since tuition fees change frequently, they are not listed.

## Continuing Education

**American University,** Division of Continuing Education, McKinley Hall, Room 153, Washington, DC 20016; 202/686-2500. American University's Professional Development Seminars are short, informal noncredit courses for working adults in which business and professional skills are stressed. Courses of interest to writers are: Layout and Design for Publication; Newsletter Writing, Newsletter Production; Promotion and Publicity; Television Scriptwriting; Brown Bag Workshop; Writing and Placing Your Own Publicity; and Technical Writing. Of special interest to freelance writers is a seminar on The Business of Consulting.

American University's American Informals are noncredit seminars and workshops taught by university faculty and working professionals and include a number of practical and creative writing courses such as: Fiction Writing; Poetry Workshop; Writing Children's Literature; Advanced Non-Fiction Workshop; Journal Writing; and Writing for Fun and Profit.

Off-campus credit courses include Publicity and Print Media, and Publicity and Audiovisual Media.

On-campus "After Five and Saturday Credit Classes" have many offerings of interest to writers including: Writing for Mass Communication; Editorial Policies and Methods; Feature Article Writing; Audio-Visual Communication; Government Reporting; Public Relations Writing; Publications Layout and Design; and Business and Economic Journalism. Literature courses include: Creative Writing and Technical Writing.

American University also presents the Visiting Writers Series of lectures, readings, and workshops sponsored by the Department of Literature. Participants have included authors Gail Godwin and Stanley Elkin. For more information on the series, call 202/686-2450.

**Catholic University,** University College, Box 75, Washington, DC 20064; 202/635-5300. Credit and noncredit courses include: Writing for Organizations; Public and Private; and Developing Writing Skills.

**Editorial Experts Inc.,** 5905 Pratt Street, Alexandria, VA 22310; 703/823-3223 days; 703/971-7350 24-hour message. For more than ten years, Editorial Experts Inc., under the direction of founder and president Laura Horowitz, has been providing hands-on editorial training to Washington businesses, groups, and agencies. EEI offers custom courses in writing, editing, production and design, and public relations, designed to meet the specific needs of a particular company or group, and it conducts instruction at client locations.

EEI offers its courses to the public on an open-registration basis. EEI schedules two sessions a year (September-December and March-June) with more than 20 classes offered each session. Courses are taught by working practitioners who provide professional-level instruction in courses designed to introduce students to new skills and help them explore career possibilities, or to enable them to develop or brush-up existing skills in order to move upward in their careers. Instruction is achieved through a combination of lecture, workshop, and exercise formats.

The courses are designed as introductions or surveys, rather than as comprehensive instruction in a subject. They are compact, briefer than programs offered in the university setting, and cover a lot of material in a short period of time.

Editorial and production courses include: A Grammar Refresher; Professional Proofreading; Introduction to Copyediting; Intermediate Editing; Technical Editing; Editorial Job Market; and Resumes That Get Editorial Jobs. Writing courses include: Writing for Clarity; Journalistic Writing; Report Writing; Proposal Writing; and Scriptwriting. Other topics are covered as well, such as typesetting, word processing, self-publishing, direct mail, and newsletters. Of particular interest is the Freelancers' Tax and Financial Seminar. (See also page 109.)

Editorial Experts is also a good source for reference materials for writers, editors, and production workers. The book division sells the course texts and materials used in class, as well as reference, style, and guide books. In addition, EEI publishes an award-winning newsletter, *The Editorial Eye*, with articles on publication and production processes·

**George Mason University,** Division of Continuing Education, 4400 University Drive, Fairfax, VA 22020; 703/323-2436. Courses in creative writing, fiction, and poetry, and in the teaching of writing.

**Georgetown University,** School for Summer and Continuing Education, Washington, DC 20057; 202/625-3003. Noncredit creative writing courses include: Writing Poems; Freelance Writing; Creative Writing; Writing Workshop; and Advanced Writing Workshop. Other courses of special interest are Tools for Research and Writing; Information Skills; and Washington Media Relations.

**Georgetown University's Annual Writers Conference,** School for Summer and Continuing Education, 306 Intercultural Center, Washington, DC 20057; 202/625-8106. Since 1959, Georgetown University has sponsored an annual Writers Conference. At each conference there is a top-flight novelist, poet, and short story writer in residence with each delivering one major presentation in a morning session. The remaining two morning sessions consist of panels in which editors, agents, and authors discuss various aspects of publishing, such as marketing and promotion procedures. In the afternoon sessions participants who have submitted manuscripts take part in workshops where guest authors and students critique works in progress. Each resident author has a Georgetown University English Department faculty member assistant to allow for personal attention to workshop participants. (Individuals without manuscripts may attend the morning sessions.)

The conferences are attended mostly by fiction writers seeking feedback—criticism and encouragement in a congenial and supportive atmosphere. Evenings are devoted to readings, cocktail hours, and social events, which are open to the public.

Katherine Anne Porter was the first keynote speaker in 1961, and subsequent participating authors have included Ann Beattie, Dan E. Moldea, James T. Farrell, Elizabeth Janeway, and Abigail McCarthy.

**Montgomery College.** Germantown Campus: 20200 Observation Drive, Germantown, MD 20874; 301/972-2000;
Rockville Campus: 51 Mannakee Street, Rockville, MD 20850; 301/279-5000;
Takoma Park Campus: Takoma Avenue and Fenton Street, Takoma Park, MD 20912; 301/587-4090. Credit and noncredit courses offered at all three campuses. Credit courses include:

Journalism; Creative Writing; Fiction; and Technical Writing. For further information call 301/279-5310. Noncredit courses include Technical Writing and Feature Stories. For information, call 301/279-5288.

**Mount Vernon College,** Continuing Education and Summer School, 2100 Foxhall Road, NW, Washington, DC 20007; 202/331-3539. Credit and noncredit courses have included: Newswriting; Speechwriting; English for Careers; The Editor's Job; Advertising and Public Relations; Publication Layout and Design.

**Northern Virginia Community College.** Alexandria Campus: 3001 North Beauregard Street, Alexandria, VA 22311; 703/323-4285;

Annandale Campus: 8333 Little River Turnpike, Annandale, VA 22003; 703/323-3000;

Woodbridge Campus: 15200 Smoketown Road, Woodbridge, VA 22191; 703/670-2191.

Courses have included: Introduction to Journalism; Technical Writing; Reporting; Creative Writing; Short Story; Editing and Make-up; Newswriting; Feature Writing; Investigative Reporting; Creative Writing; Creative Short Story Writing; Creative Poetry Writing. Northern Virginia Community College also offers Community Service (noncredit) courses such as Coping With Writing Anxiety, and Revising and Editing, at the Annandale campus, and Getting Published Fast, at the Alexandria campus.

**Open University,** 3333 Connecticut Avenue, NW, Washington, DC 20008; 202/966-9606. Organized in 1975 with a schedule of 24 classes, Open University now offers 300 classes six times a year in two-month sessions. Instruction at "Open U" is casual, with many classes taught in the instructors' homes. The aim of Open U is to allow individuals to gain experience in an area of interest without the pressure of grades or the limitations of long-term commitments. Open U sees itself as a springboard for students into new interests or careers, which they can then pursue in greater detail at another institution or on their own.

Open U has a core of courses that remains constant, but new

courses are added every two months, and courses often appear and reappear in rotating sessions.

One of the most appealing features of Open University is that its catalogs boast useful and unusual courses which frequently are not available elsewhere, such as Copyright, which guides students through the maze of rules and regulations pertaining to copyright protection, or Strategies for Overcoming Writer's Block, a six-week workshop taught by a psychologist. Other courses include: The Short Story; Playwriting; Journal Writing; Romance Writing; TV and Film Scriptwriting; Self-Publishing; Freelance Opportunities in D.C.; Getting Published in Magazines; Book Reviewing; Writing a Novel to Sell; and dozens of other writing and writing-related courses. Open U also has courses useful to writers in such subjects as business, photography, word processing, and graphics.

**Prince George's Community College,** 301 Largo Road, Largo, MD 20772, credit course information: 301/322-0866; non-credit course information: 301/322-0875. Credit courses include: Grammar; Editing; Introduction to Freelance Writing; Technical Writing; Creative Writing; Introduction to Journalism; and Newspaper Laboratory. Noncredit courses include: Proofreading; Editing; and Report Writing.

**University of Maryland,** College Park, Maryland. Academic Advisement: 301/454-4044; Evening and Weekend Credit Courses: 301/454-5735; Noncredit Short Courses: 301/454-4712; Open University Credit Courses: 301/454-2765. Credit and noncredit courses are offered in creative writing, technical writing, and journalism.

**University of Virginia,** Falls Church Regional Center, Department of Continuing Education, 2990 Telestan Court, Falls Church, VA 22042; 703/698-5171. Courses in Creative Writing; Journal Writing; Thoughts on Paper; and Poetry Writing.

**U.S. Department of Agriculture, Graduate School,** 600 Maryland Avenue, SW, Washington, DC 20024; 202/447-4419. The USDA Graduate School, in addition to its Certificate Program in Editorial Practices (see Certificate Programs, below), offers a wide range of credit and noncredit courses in Mass Communications, Graphics, and Photography, including: Reporting for the Print Media; Feature Writing; Photojournalism; Audiovisual Communications; Media Relations; Critical Writing; Government Writing; Humor Writing; and Practical Writing.

**Washington Education Press Association,** 1710 Connecticut Avenue, NW, Washington, DC 20009; 202/797-2108. Washington Edpress is a professional organization of editors, writers, artists, executives, information specialists, and production people associated with education journalism in the nation's capital. (Education, in the context of Edpress, has a broad definition.)

Edpress conducts an annual conference in May or June highlighted by discussions and workshops on topics related to writing, editing, and production. Past speakers have included Norman Cousins and Nat Hentoff. Edpress also runs informal meetings to expand professional development skills and share resources with members. In addition, it conducts an informal and unofficial support group for freelance writers and consultants, which meets once a month to discuss such matters as how to set prices and promote skills. All activities of Edpress are open to members and nonmembers.

**Washington Independent Writers,** 525 National Press Building, Washington, DC 20045; 202/347-4973. Among its services, Washington Independent Writers offers a variety of educational programs to its members and the community at large. Monthly workshops include panel discussions of such topics as: the business of writing, syndication, romance writing, selling yourself, writing for cable TV, financial planning, and political reporting. All-day conferences have included Writing Strategies for the '80s, Preparing for the Communications Revolution, and Making it as a Freelance Writer in Good Times and Bad.

**The Washington School,** 1901 Q Street, NW, Washington, DC 20009; 202/234-9382. The Washington School is the educational center of the Institute for Policy Studies. It offers a number of courses in journalism, primarily in investigative reporting. Past courses have included Foreign Reporting, Creative Journalism, and Speechwriting. While courses are geared to develop professional skills, at the same time they examine the role that journalism plays in opinion-forming and public policy-making.

**The Writer's Center,** 4800 Sangamore Road, Bethesda, MD 20816; 301/229-0930. A nonprofit organization of writers, designers, small-press publishers, and literature enthusiasts, this active and diverse group arranges a number of special programs including: a Visiting Writers Series in which resident authors hold readings and workshops in poetry and fiction for one week; readings of poetry and fiction by local and well-known visiting authors; plays in progress; and conferences on various subjects of interest to writers.

In addition, the center offers a wide range of workshops for beginning and advanced writers of fiction and nonfiction and production workers. These courses, of a generalized, specialized, and experimental nature, are professionally oriented and aim to sharpen the writer's critical eye. Courses and workshops are offered in poetry, comedy, playwriting, creative writing, creative writing for young people, beginning the novel, short story writing, science fiction, mystery, adventure, and fantasy, feature writing, creative journalism, freelancing, journal writing, and criticism. Also offered are workshops in autobiography, dialogue, the creative use of punctuation, and editing fiction and nonfiction.

Writers involved in producing collateral materials will find the center's production workshops extremely valuable: Getting it Printed; Making it Camera Ready; Hands-on Offset; Typesetting; and Word Processing. (After taking production courses and demonstrating proficiency in the use of the Center's typesetting, printing, and word processing equipment, students may then rent that equipment for their own use.)

# Certificate Programs

## George Washington University, Publication Specialist Program, Center for Continuing Education in Washington, 801 22nd Street, NW, Washington, DC 20052; 202/676-7273.

Clearly the most ambitious of the certificate programs is George Washington University's Publication Specialist Program, which has been successfully training students to compete and excel in the local marketplace for eight years. The Publication Specialist Program offers the most intensive and comprehensive instruction available in the metropolitan area for those who aspire to a career in any facet of publishing.

While other programs and schools offer an introduction to the subject, the Publication Specialist Program has more to offer the student already committed to a career in or related to publishing, and in turn it expects and demands more from participants. Successful completion of the program requires talent, hard work, and a considerable amount of time devoted to out-of-class assignments and study.

The program is designed to equip students to go out into the marketplace and break into new fields or to broaden the horizons of those already in publishing positions. The courses of vocational training are geared to publishing specialties as they are practiced in the Washington area. Students are taught the fundamentals of writing and rewriting, editing, proofreading, design, print processes, and management as they apply to the production of magazines, books, newsletters, brochures, and audiovisual materials.

Students can participate in the one-year, noncredit, graduate program on an open enrollment basis or they may apply for certificate-candidate status. A certificate is awarded after the successful completion of 240 instruction hours in a total of ten courses, six required and four elective. Graduate status is not strictly required for admission to the program, but two years of college and one year of professional experience are preferred. Two 16-week sessions and a summer session make up the program, with each 16-week semester divided into two eight-week sessions. Classes meet evenings or Saturday mornings once a week for eight weeks.

Courses include: Proofreading and Copyediting; Graphic Tools and Techniques; Intermediate Editing; Principles of Marketing; Printing and the Graphic Arts; Association Publishing; Computer Publishing; Audiovisual Publishing; Technical Editing; Publications Finance and Accounting; and many more.

After completing the program, students should be familiar with all aspects of book and magazine publishing processes and will be equipped to carry out projects from conception through production to financing and management.

For more information, program brochures are available from the Publication Specialist Program office, and information sessions describing the program, requirements, tuition, application, and registration procedures are held monthy.

### Georgetown University, Certificate Program in Editing and Publications, School for Summer and Continuing Education, Washington, DC 20057; 202/625-3003.

Georgetown University's Certificate Program in Editing and Publications consists of four courses designed to give students a broad spectrum of practical experience in the editorial fields. Courses are taught by working professionals who provide program participants with the necessary background to break into a particular field of publishing and offer those who are already working in their fields skills to aid in advancement. The program instruction, carried out through lectures, field trips, and practical exercises, aims to touch upon all facets of publication processes as they pertain to newsletters, press releases, brochures, reports, and magazines. Principles of Writing and Editing, Developing Resource Skills, Advanced Editing, and Graphic Design and Printing comprise the program sequence. Admission to this graduate level program requires a bachelor's degree, but in certain cases professional experience may substitute for the B.A. requirement. (Courses can be taken by noncertificate candidates as space allows.)

The university's School for Summer and Continuing Education also provides in-house training to interested organizations and will tailor programs to specific needs.

### U.S. Department of Agriculture, Graduate School, 600 Maryland Avenue, SW, Room 129, Washington, DC 20024; 202/447-5885. The USDA Graduate School was established 60

years ago by the Department of Agriculture to provide continuing education for research scientists. It has since evolved to provide a wide range of courses intended primarily for government personnel, but open to all individuals with or without graduate status. Also, the Graduate School, like Georgetown Unversity and Editorial Experts Inc., custom designs courses for interested groups.

The curriculum for programs leading to the Certificate of Accomplishment in Editorial Practices is designed by the client community, including federal management personnel who employ writers, editors, and production workers. It therefore has a practical and professional orientation and seeks to train individuals for the editorial marketplace through a combination of workshops, institutes, lectures, and seminars. Courses generally meet one evening a week for ten weeks in four sessions each year.

Courses include: Principles of Editing and their Application; Proofreading; Intermediate Editing; Principles of Layout and Design; Technical Editing; Indexing; and Publications Management. (Certificate programs are also available in Graphic Arts and Mass Communications.)

This is by no means a comprehensive list of educational resources for writers, but rather a starting point. Educational opportunities are offered by different groups in ever greater numbers and varieties. Many unstructured and informal learning activities and skills workshops are offered regularly by local businesses and trade associations. Membership in professional organizations is an excellent way to stay on top of new developments and, by scanning the trade newsletters, you'll find notices of upcoming conferences and seminars. And keep an eye on "Washington Business," the business section of *The Washington Post,* appearing each Monday. It lists a weekly calendar of meetings, conferences, and seminars, many of interest to writers and editors. Frequently listed are courses of use to freelance writers concerning taxes, financial planning, setting up a consulting business, and marketing.

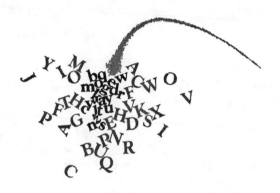

# Writers' Organizations

## Patricia Rankin and Kitty Stone

**W**riters who are pursuing careers on their own—whether from a corner of the living room, a den turned into an office, or rented space downtown—often feel isolated. Organizations that are devoted to their interests or that provide a chance to talk with other writers who understand such ailments as writer's block offer a welcome lift. Anyone who writes fulltime for pay or in hope of turning out *the* great novel spends a vast amount of time cutting away from the rest of the world and concentrating, concentrating, concentrating on the pages slowly taking shape. Writers' organizations help members to feel less isolated, more in touch, when they look up from their work.

Washington is rich in organizations that will help a writer to strengthen the craft, make contacts, find friends, keep up to date, or learn what has come before. Writers' organizations provide opportunities to dabble, to become involved, to run the show.

*Patricia Rankin is a staff writer for the National Association of Homebuilders and does freelance writing on business and travel. Kitty Stone is the Assistant to the Executive Director of WIW. She is a graduate of The George Washington University and writes for the WIW Newsletter.*

Some groups are national in scope, others are national with local chapters in the Washington area, some are local in origin and emphasis.

**American Medical Writers Association,** 5272 River Road, Suite 410, Bethesda, MD 20816; 301/986-9119. The association was founded in 1940 and now has 12 chapters and approximately 1,800 members. It is dedicated to the advancement and improvement of medical communications, and its members include medical writers, editors, publishers, and photographers. Members receive the national and chapter newsletters, a quarterly journal, *Medical Communications,* the opportunity to use a job placement exchange, and the chance to be listed in the AMWA membership directory. Members may join specific sections (e.g., public relations, editing, freelance writing) and attend workshops and seminars focused on these topics.

**The Capital Press Club,** P.O. Box 19403, Washington, DC 20036. The Capital Press Club is an organization dedicated to improving opportunities for and images of minorities in communications. Members work in print, radio and television, advertising, and public relations. The group holds free regular membership meetings featuring major figures and issues in the news. Members receive the CPC newsletter, the *Capital Communicator.*

**Capital Press Women,** c/o E. Bruce Harrison Company, 605 14th Street, NW, Washington, DC 20005; 202/638-1200. Capital Press Women, an affiliate of the National Federation of Press Women, was organized in 1973. Members of the NPFW are professional communicators from all segments of the media. There are approximately 50 chapters of the organization that include more than 5,000 members.

Capital Press Women runs monthly meetings and annual conferences directed at skills development. A vital aspect of the group is the opportunity to talk with peers and build a network of associates.

The NPFW provides a national writing contest for members and for high school students, a monthly magazine called *PressWoman,* a Woman of Achievement awards program, and scholarships. Membership in Capital Press Women is open to professionals involved in any area of the communications field for at least a year immediately prior to application.

**Cultural Alliance of Greater Washington,** 633 E Street, NW, Washington, DC 20004; 202/638-2406. The Alliance is dedicated to developing communication among its membership. Its goals are to provide services to members and to advocate the collective interests of members in order to create an understanding of the arts in the community. The Alliance was formed in 1978 and now has over 200 member organizations and 550 individual members. The Alliance offers its members a monthly calendar of local arts events, discounts on group purchasing, a group health insurance plan, a *Washington Cultural Directory*, and a resume file.

**National Association of Government Communicators,** P.O. Box 7127, Alexandria, VA 22307; 703/768-4546. The association was formed in 1976 through a merger of the Federal Editors Association and the Government Information Organization. The largest chapter of the group is in Washington, D.C., which has more than half of the approximate 1,000 national members. NAGC members receive a monthly newsletter, *NAGC Communicator,* may attend monthly luncheon meetings with speakers, and may participate in a job clearinghouse. The organization sponsors awards programs to honor excellence in government communication. Active membership is open to writers who are seeking to be employed or who are employed by local, state, or federal government.

**National Press Club,** National Press Building, Washington, DC 20045; 202/737-2500. The National Press Club, founded in 1908 and grown to over 4,500 members, is the nation's oldest and largest press club. The Club offers a wide range of services to its members. Members can hear and question heads of state, cabinet officials, and other newsmakers at the more than 60 Club luncheons every year. The Club also offers a job referral service, a travel program, an active arts and cultural affairs program, a reference library, an awards program, and a monthly newsletter.

**National Writers Union, D.C. Chapter,** 919 6th Street, NW, Washington, DC 20001; 202/289-1123. The Organizing Committee for a National Writers Union was conceived at the 1981 meeting of the American Writers Congress in New York. There are approximately 1,300 members in 12 cities across the country. The purpose of the organization is to use collective bargaining techniques to promote writers' rights and to improve contract conditions with publishers. Members receive the national newsletter, *The American Writer,* and the local newsletter, *The Washington Writer.* Membership is divided into four categories—nonfiction books, journalism, fiction books, and poetry and small press.

**Society for Technical Communication,** 815 15th Street, NW, Suite 506, Washington, DC 20005; 202/737-0035. The society is a professional organization for technical communicators. It allows its members, who are involved in every aspect of the technical communication field, to exchange ideas and information about that field. STC is devoted to the education, improvement, and advancement of its members. Members receive the STC journal, *Technical Communication,* and the newsletter, *INTERCOM.*

**Society of American Travel Writers,** 1120 Connecticut Avenue, NW, Suite 940, Washington, DC 20036; 202/785-5567. The Society of American Travel Writers, founded in 1956, is a nonprofit organization for approximately 700 people involved in the travel industry. Its purpose is to educate and assist both the traveling public and travel writers, editors, broadcasters, photographers, and public relations executives. Members receive the newsletter, *The Travel Writer,* and may attend workshops and conventions around the world. Membership is by invitation.

**Society of Professional Journalists, Sigma Delta Chi,** Washington Professional Chapter, P.O. Box 19555, Washington, DC 20036. This is the oldest and largest organization for journalists in the country, with almost 30,000 members nationwide. The group was founded in 1909 and now has over 300 professional and campus chapters. The purposes of the society are to recognize outstanding achievement by journalists, advance high ethical standards in the profession, and elevate the prestige of journalism. The organization is actively involved in protecting First Amendment rights. Members receive the monthly magazine, *The Quill*, a local newsletter, and the opportunity to attend monthly meetings on issues of concern to journalists. Professional members must be working journalists or teachers of journalism and must have one year's experience in the field.

**Washington Area Film/Video League,** 418 7th Street, NW, Washington, DC 20004; 202/783-0400. This organization was established in 1975 as a clearinghouse for information about film and video in the Washington metropolitan area. WAF/VL offers its 300 members monthly program meetings, the monthly *WAF/VL Newsletter*, workshops, a membership directory, and the opportunity to get together with filmmakers to discuss what is new and what is needed in the film industry. Membership is open to anyone interested in film and video.

**Washington Area Writers,** 3015 Graham Road, Falls Church, VA 22042; 703/560-0040. Washington Area Writers was formed in 1972 and has approximately 60 members. The organization holds monthly meetings with speakers on a variety of topics, and it produces a monthly newsletter for its members. WAW members are encouraged to exchange ideas and talk informally following programs.

**Washington Education Press Association,** 1710 Connecticut Avenue, NW, Washington, DC 20009; 202/797-2108. Washington Edpress was founded in 1959 so that education writers in the area could share the skills and information needed to make them professional writers. Edpress' 200 members receive the monthly *Edpress Express*, reduced prices for monthly luncheon programs, admission to brown bag workshops, and access to the job clearinghouse. The organization holds an annual awards competition and publishes a bi-annual salary survey for fulltime and freelance education writers.

**Washington Independent Writers,** 525 National Press Building, Washington, DC 20045; 202/347-4973. WIW is a professional association for 1,400 freelance writers in the

Washington, D.C., area. WIW members, from beginners to experienced writers, share an interest in continuing to improve their skills and in working to better the conditions of their profession. Members receive the monthly *WIW Newsletter*, may attend monthly workshops on various aspects of writing, use the Job Bank, participate in group health and legal plans, and take part in the social events and small group meetings sponsored by the organization. WIW conducts an annual writers conference, which members may attend at a discount price.

**Washington Press Club,** 1330 New Hampshire Avenue, NW, Washington, DC 20036; 202/296-5062. The Washington Press Club was created in 1919 as the Women's National Press Club because women were not admitted into the National Press Club. In 1971, the organization changed its name and allowed men to become members. (The National Press Club now admits women.) The Washington Press Club now has approximately 700 members, half of whom are male. The purpose of the club is to encourage professional standards for journalists. The organization sponsors seminars and workshops on topics of national and international interest. Prospective members must meet exacting standards and be sponsored by two active members of the Club.

**Washington Romance Writers,** 3727 Chesapeake Street, NW, Washington, DC 20016; 202/363-1499. Washington Romance Writers was organized in 1982 and is a chapter of the Romance Writers of America. The national organization has more than 1,400 members; the Washington group has approximately 90. WRW usually holds meetings twice a month in members' homes to allow romance writers to meet and exchange ideas on this specialized field. Members receive *The Washington Romance Writers Newsletter*, a monthly that provides information on markets, events, and developments in romance writing. Membership is open to anyone.

**Women In Communications Inc.,** Washington, D.C. Professional Chapter, 3052 South Abingdon Street, Arlington, VA 22206; 703/998-7307. This is one of the oldest communications organizations in the country with nearly 10,000 members nationwide and 325 members locally. The Washington,

D.C. Professional Chapter of WICI provides its members, men and women from all fields of the communications industry, with a support group and offers opportunities for friendships and professional development. The purpose of WICI is to work for a free and responsible press, to unite men and women communicators and recognize their achievements, to maintain high professional communications standards, and to encourage members to pursue their individual and collective efforts. Washington WICI issues a monthly newsletter, maintains a job network, sponsors monthly programs, and monitors legislation affecting communicators.

**Women In Film and Video,** Friendship Station, P.O. Box 39049, Washington, DC 20016. Women in Film and Video was founded in 1979 by and for women interested in filmmaking. Its 250 members include professionals in all areas of the film industry: producers, directors, technicians, researchers, and distributors, as well as writers. The organization offers educational workshops, screenings, and social events, and sponsors the bi-annual Women's Film Festival. WIFV is particularly involved in working to increase recognition of women in film and provides its members with opportunities to make contacts with filmmakers from around the world. Members receive the WIFV newsletter every other month.

**Women's National Book Association,** Washington/Baltimore Chapter, P.O. Box 57102, Washington, DC 20037. The association, founded in 1917, is an organization for both men and women dedicated to the book and publishing industries. There are approximately 60 members in the Washington/Baltimore chapter, including authors, publishers, agents, illustrators, librarians, and booksellers. Members meet regularly for luncheons, publishing seminars, and discussion groups, and receive a membership directory and the national and local newsletters. WNBA Washington/Baltimore offers its members the opportunity to expand their social and professional networks nationwide.

**The Writer's Center,** 4800 Sangamore Road, Bethesda, MD 20816; 301/229-0930. The Writer's Center is a nonprofit organization for writers of all levels and genres. Its 1,300 members include small press publishers and graphic artists, as well as writers and editors. The Center's goal is to help the general public participate in the creation, distribution, and enjoyment of literature and the graphic arts. To this end, the Center offers courses on every aspect of writing and graphic design, allows its members access to typesetting and printing equipment, and operates the Book Gallery, which handles magazines and books by local writers and small press publishers. Members receive the bimonthly newsletter, *Carousel*, and discounts on events and purchases.

**The Writers' League of Washington,** 9709 Lorain Avenue, Silver Spring, MD 20901; 301/589-0810. The Writers' League of Washington was formed in 1917 and is one of the oldest writers' groups in the area. The organization's 35 members meet once a month between October and May at the Chevy Chase Library to hear speakers and exchange reactions to each others' work. A different literary form is discussed each month, from book reviews to poetry. Members receive the monthly newsletter, *The Write Way*. The Writers' League also has smaller group meetings on specialized topics and sponsors writing contests for members only. To become a member, one must attend two meetings, submit writing samples, and pay the annual dues.

# The Writer
# At Leisure

Writing need not be all work and no play. In this final section
we try to remind the Washington writer that this is a city filled
with delights to revive the spirit and refuel the creative process.
A writer in need of reflection may seek the Matisse Tower or
the Bishop's Garden. One seeking stimulation rather than repose
might watch a play at Arena Stage or drink champagne in the
lounge atop the Kennedy Center. Writers have always looked
to those who came before for inspiration. Literary landmarks
ranging from the library built to honor the giant of English
literature—William Shakespeare—to the grave of Scott and Zelda
Fitzgerald serve as reminders of what the written word may accomplish. We encourage the reader to "loaf and invite the soul."

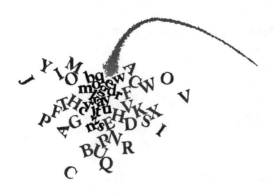

# Creative Retreats and Literary Landmarks

## Rosemary Beavers

You've been sitting in the Main Reading Room of the Library of Congress for days—months—years. The computer is down. Your shelf of books has been emptied. Your application for a desk has been lost. You have tried sitting under the history pillar and staring at the law pillar. You've reversed that. You have wandered into the bathrooms off the Great Hall (the best public bathrooms in Washington) to stare at the ceiling murals. You have begun to look forward to lunch in the cafeteria. Yes, you have all the symptoms. You need a creative retreat. Something to take your mind off writing. Especially all the writing you haven't yet done.

Walk out the front door of the library. Turn right. Walk over to Massachusetts Avenue, to Bob's Famous, for an ice cream cone. Oreo and Chocolate Moose, covered with jimmies (or crushed Heath bars, or sno-caps) will help. Right across the street is the American Cafe, with buttery croissants and elegant take-

---

*Rosemary Beavers has lived in Washington longer than any place except New Jersey. She works as a writer for the federal government and is a recent convert to opera. She is a member of Poor House Writers.*

out food. Clutching this haul, walk to any nearby park, sit under a tree, and watch lawmakers and breakers pass by.

Or, walk out the front door of the library and turn left. Walk one block to Pennsylvania Avenue and into the Hawk 'n Dove. Drink. Walk further up Pennsylvania Avenue to Seventh Street. Turn left, walk a block to Eastern Market, home of the best crab cakes around (closed Mondays). Walk north on Seventh Street to East Capitol Street and back up East Capitol to the library. You've just killed a couple of hours. Maybe now you'll be ready for the library.

## Gardens

The closest park to the Library of Congress is the Capitol grounds. Sit anywhere and contemplate the Capitol Building. Sure, some of its inhabitants may not charm you, but the building is lovely. If you could live in it, which room would you want? This decision may take hours. The quietest part of the grounds is the Grotto, on the Senate (north) side. Designed by Frederick Law Olmstead, it has brick walls and a tile roof to shade the benches around its edges. It is a cool place on even the hottest day.

As long as you're on the west side of the Capitol, walk over to the Botanical Garden Conservatory on Maryland Avenue. It may convince you that there's a topiary in your future. The Bartholdi Fountain, just across from Independence Avenue, is an ornate cast iron fountain designed by the creator of the Statue of Liberty. Surrounded by gardens, it is a lovely contrast to the squat Rayburn House Office Building next door.

Constitution Gardens, northwest of the Washington Monument, has a lake with islands, benches, and few people compared to the rest of the Mall. The stunning Vietnam Memorial, just west of the gardens, draws you into it; after you've seen it, you need to walk on, up to the Lincoln Memorial. You may not have been there since Aunt Em visited from Kansas. Try it—sit on the steps and stare at beautiful Washington. You may also sit on the steps of the Jefferson Memorial—and, as long as it isn't cherry blossom season, there will be fewer people around.

If you've been working at the National Archives (especially if you have been reading microfilm) you will be desperate to get outside. Of course you can just sit on the Mall, or go ice-skating in the winter. But you may also go to the Hirshhorn Sculpture Garden, sit near the pool and willow tree and let your mind wander. Give up research and write a novel about the Burghers of Calais. Or walk up to the National Museum of American Art/National Portrait Gallery (9th and F Streets, NW). It has the best courtyard in Washington. If it isn't lunchtime, you will probably sit there all alone.

Georgetown has several small parks, some overwhelmed with children and dogs. For quiet, the garden at the Old Stone House (3031 M Street, NW) is close to unbeatable—except in the middle of summer, when the exhaust, noise, and heat of passing cars will turn a thoughtful writer to thoughts of violence. But it is lovely in tulip season. And there are plenty of bars nearby.

The gardens at Dumbarton Oaks (31st and R Streets, NW), with 16 acres of flowering trees and plants, were designed by Beatrix Farrand, and are often compared to the great gardens of Europe. Open daily, admission to the gardens is free from November to March, but will cost you a dollar from April to October. If the gardens are closed when you get there, just walk on down R Street to Oak Hill Cemetery.

Besides Oak Hill Cemetery, two other cemeteries invite creative retreats. Rock Creek Cemetery, on Rock Creek Church Road (near North Capitol Street), has many Victorian monuments, and one of the most beautiful statues anywhere— the Adams Memorial. And Congressional Cemetery (18th and E Streets, SE) has many historic graves, including those of John Philip Sousa and of a Choctaw Indian chief, and lots of spots for peaceful thoughts.

For those who crave escape to near-wilderness, Rock Creek Park, with its 1,800 acres right in the heart of Northwest Washington, provides it. Secluded paths allow even sedentary writers the opportunity to hike, to jog, to ride horseback, or merely to picnic along the stream. Don't forget Theodore Roosevelt Island. Only ten minutes from downtown and within sight of the Watergate and the Kennedy Center, Theodore Roosevelt Island is a wildlife sanctuary and an attractive place for hiking or picnicking. It may be reached by car, bicycle, or foot from the Virginia side, or by canoe.

Finally, there is the Bishop's Garden at the Washington

Cathedral. Very organized, with labeled plants, it is walled in, full of benches, and has a covered gazebo for rainy days. It's best on weekends and in late afternoon. You can stare at the Cathedral, buy herbs, and plan your formal garden—which you will create with the royalties from the book you have been organizing all this time.

# Refuge

There are times when you can't walk or sit outside. You would like to sit somewhere, other than a library, in pleasant surroundings, to write or to plan to write. Here are some suggestions.

The Smithsonian, that wonderful complex of buildings, is so busy that musing on writer's block is difficult. But try the Matisse Tower of the National Gallery of Art's East Wing. It isn't always open, but when it is, it is usually quiet. Matisse did those cutouts near the end of his life, so surely you can wait another day to write your next chapter. The National Gallery is also one of the very few museums with real telephone booths. You can sit down, close the door, and call your agent.

The entire Freer Gallery is usually deserted. It has a central courtyard surrounded by galleries. Sit in the Peacock Room, and if you can't decide what to write next, at least you can take sides in the dispute. Of course it is beautiful—but would you want to eat breakfast in it? Again, such decisions can take hours.

Away from the Mall and closer to the White House, the Renwick Gallery's Grand Salon has paintings to stare at and little tables to write on. The cafeteria on the Roof Terrace at the Kennedy Center provides views of the city and the river. Buy a cup of coffee and study the bright batiks. If the place isn't busy, you can stay all afternoon.

The Phillips Collection (1600 21st Street, NW) has some comfortable chairs and quiet rooms. Picture yourself part of the boating party. Dream away the day, occasionally jotting down a thought. Then walk over to Dupont Circle for food, drink, books, records, and a general return to the real world. Perhaps the royalties from your second book (the royalties from the first are going to the garden) might go to organizing your own boating party down the Potomac.

Not everybody approves of zoos, but watching animals can

# Good Guidebooks

Should you feel the need of additional guidance, here are some general and specialized guides to Washington:

**General**

The best of the all-round guidebooks—those showing where to go, how to get there—are Marilyn J. Appleberg's *I Love Washington Guide* (Collier, $4.95), and *The Washington Post Guide to Washington* (McGraw-Hill, $5.95). Both are lively and thorough.

*Washington Itself: An informal guide to the capital of the United States* by E.J. Applewhite (New York: Alfred A. Knopf, 1981; $8.95), while not a guidebook in the usual sense, is perhaps the best book available for the serious student of the city. The author's purpose is "to provide fresh descriptions of the buildings, museums, and monuments of the nation's capital in terms of the social and esthetic values of the 1980s." He succeeds admirably; his is a beautiful book in both form and content.

**Food**

*Best Restaurants (& Others): Washington, D.C. and Environs* by Phyllis C. Richman (101 Productions, $4.95). Richman, executive food editor and restaurant critic of *The Washington Post*, surveys culinary Washington with a witty and practiced hand. Menus included.

**Nature**

*Natural Washington* by Bill and Phyllis Thomas (Holt, Rinehart and Winston, $6.95) is a superbly written and illustrated exploration of "wild places"—parks, gardens, trails, etc.—within a 50-mile radius of Washington.

*City of Trees: The Complete Botanical and Historical Guide to the Trees of Washington, D.C.* by Melanie Choukas-Bradley and Polly Alexander (Acropolis Books, 1981, $24.95). A stunning combination of history and botany, with outstanding photographs and illustrations.

*—Thomazine Shanahan*

be restful. The National Zoological Park (3001 Connecticut Avenue, NW) is full of them. Admire the birds in their unusual aviary, or stare at the seals cavorting in their pool. Remember that animal books frequently make the bestseller list.

Go back to Washington Cathedral. Go up to the Pilgrim Gallery for the best view of the city. There are stone benches and almost nobody around. Or pick a little side chapel and stare at a stained-glass window. Except for an occasional tour, silence is total. Remember—the Cathedral has been "in process" for 75 years. Take the long view.

## Cheap Thrills

After working on your latest draft of the history of buttonholing, you need to rest. You have visited gardens, studied statues, and now you want to be entertained. Your royalties haven't yet arrived. What you need are some cheap thrills.

Check with the Kennedy Center to see if they are selling standing room for any of their productions. It's impossible to tell without asking—sometimes they sell SRO tickets to shows that are not sold out, but sometimes they don't sell it even if a show *is* sold out. Perhaps the policy is based on phases of the moon. But it is possible to see a Washington Opera production for more than 75 percent less than it cost the people sitting in the row you were standing behind. And if you bought a Watergate pastry (among the best) and a roast beef and cole slaw on pumpernickel from the Watergate deli, you could eat well, sit and wait for tickets to go on sale, meet interesting people in the line, and see a ballet or an original play almost within your budget.

Of course this takes time. If you want to see Pavarotti or Baryshnikov, it might take a very long time. If you can afford to just buy a ticket, you will save time. But if you want to forget writing and get a change of scene, spend some time waiting in lines. Wait in line for half-price tickets at TICKETplace (12th and F Streets, NW), munching on a blueberry doughnut from Reeves Bakery (1209 F Street, NW) to help the time go by. Get up early on Monday morning and stand in line outside the Performing Arts Society (Jordan Kitt's) for Library of Congress chamber music tickets. At 25 cents apiece, they are hard to beat. Or wait in line to get into the National Gallery of Art concerts on Sunday nights—they're free. And all the people you meet can be characters in your next novel.

Some events or places are not so expensive, and you don't usually need to wait in lines. Performances at Arena Stage and the Folger Theatre are usually cheaper than productions at the Kennedy Center. The Kennedy Center Concert Hall has obstructed view seats for under five dollars, and if you sit in the front row and lean forward you will be able to see most of the stage. The Washington Ballet performs at Lisner Auditorium. Its prices are reasonable, and the choreography is often outstanding. One Step Down has open mike (no cover) on Saturday afternoons. Both the Kennedy Center and Washington Cathedral have organ demonstrations. Throughout the year, the Kennedy Center has free presentations. Scan the entertainment sections of Washington newspapers.

Go to the Circle Theatre. Whether it's to see *Breaker Morant* and *Gallipoli* or *Mommie Dearest* and *Polyester*, you will pay two dollars and be inside for hours. (You can cut the price in half: ten tickets for ten dollars.) The Biograph shows old movies and offbeat festivals of films. And the American Film Institute shows films in the best prints available. So go to the Kennedy Center for a noon lecture or National Town Meeting, check for standing room or obstructed view seats, ponder your writing in the cafeteria, go to a movie at AFI, and then to a performance in one of the theatres. An entire day used up, and you never had to go outside.

Washington has lots of free events. Of course the White House and the Cathedral are open all year, and you can tour the White House grounds two weekends a year in the fall and spring. The Cathedral has a big birthday bash and open house in the fall, when you can climb the tower—up hundreds of winding stone stairs to the bells, which ring while you are there. Dorothy Sayers was right—nine tailors could kill you. The Smithsonian has a kite festival and a frisbee festival. There is the Folklife Festival every summer on the Mall with food, crafts, music, and demonstrations. There are huge celebrations for Christmas and the Fourth of July. You can count on fireworks on the Fourth but there are fireworks other times too—to celebrate the visit of a foreign head of state or the opening of an exhibit, for example. So sit on the Capitol steps, surrounded by screaming children, marvel at the fireworks, and plot how you will get home when it's all over.

The National Symphony Orchestra has free concerts on the west lawn of the Capitol four times a summer. The various service bands have concerts at the Jefferson Memorial and at the

Capitol. There are concerts along the canal, near the Foundry in Georgetown. As long as you're near the canal, rent a boat and paddle on the canal or on the Potomac. Or ride your bike to Ohio on the canal towpath.

Just remember—the idea is to relax, take your mind off writing, and not spend too much money. Be creative—after all, you can drink champagne and order pressed duck once your bestseller is published.

## New Arrivals

Washington has lots of transients—tourists, presidents, members of Congress, researchers. But Washington, contrary to reports elsewhere, also has many people who were born here and know their way around. Of course, it would be exhilarating to arrive by helicopter on the South Lawn of the White House, but ordinary people will answer your questions on the street nevertheless, and sometimes they even say good morning.

If you don't know where to stay, get a guide from the D.C. Convention and Visitors Association (1575 I Street, NW, Washington, DC 20005). If you plan to come in the spring (cherry blossom season), expect to make a reservation and pay more for a hotel. Try to get out of a hotel quickly, as they are expensive. Bed and breakfast organizations, such as the Bed and Breakfast League Ltd. (2855 29th Street, NW, Washington, DC 20008; 202/232-8718), offer lodgings at a third to half of current hotel rates and start you off with a continental breakfast. Look in the papers or contact local university housing offices for good deals; you may be able to housesit for a family summering at the Vineyard. The Gralyn Hotel and the Tabard Inn, both on N Street, NW (off Connecticut Avenue) are attractive, small, and relatively inexpensive. But still—try to find another option— don't you know *anyone* in Washington? (Your ex-spouse's cousin?) You don't need much room, since you'll be writing else-where or wandering around lost.

Lost? What you need is a map. The D.C. Department of Transportation has an excellent free one, available during business hours (Room 519, Presidential Building, 415 12th Street, NW). The Convention and Visitors Association also has maps, and so does the Smithsonian. Remember to pay attention to the quadrants of the city: Northwest, Northeast, Southwest, Southeast. Once you realize that the District is divided into four parts, it's easy. Except for the diagonal avenues. And the circles. And that there is no J Street, but there is an Eye and a Que. See? Simple. Just settle in and make yourself comfortable.

If you arrive in August, it will be impossible to make yourself comfortable. If you have never lived in a tropical swamp before, you may not realize that just because the humidity is 100 percent does not mean that it will rain. Not even when the temperature is also 100. And this brings us to Washington's major drawback as a city—*no beach.* But you can wade in the fountains, swim in one of several free pools, and lie in a chaise lounge on the roof of your apartment building. The best bet is to cultivate people with summer homes. The rest of the seasons are not so bad—and spring and fall can be spectacular. After you have been here several years, the tiny gradations in August temperatures will make you feel good (well, at least better) as you realize that it's almost over and it's never been as bad as it was three years ago. . . .

Need a guide (besides this one of course)? There are lots to choose from. *The Washington Post Guide to Washington,* edited by Laura L. Babb, covers everything. If you want to eat, read *Best Restaurants (& Others): Washington, D.C. & Environs* by Phyllis C. Richman. Once you know where you are and where to eat, you can branch out—to *City of Trees* by Melanie Choukas-Bradley and Polly Alexander. Many of Washington's parks have labels on the trees, but if you find a tree without one, you can look it up. *Washington, D.C. Walking Tours,* by Tony P. Wrenn, and *Washington on Foot: 23 Walking Tours of Washington, D.C., Old Town Alexandria, Va., and Historic Annapolis, Md.,* edited by Allan A. Hodges and Carol A. Hodges, are both very useful if you are interested in architecture or historic preservation. And if you want to know what in the world that statue is, just look it up in *The Outdoor Sculpture of Washington, D.C.,* by James M. Goode. You'll discover that it is James Buchanan. Or Joan of Arc. They are both in Meridian Hill Park. And Joan of Arc is "noteworthy as a gift from the women of France to the women of the United States." Wonderful book.

You will want to know what's going on in Washington. *The Washington Post* lists the activities of Congress and the

Supreme Court when thay are in session. The *Post* also publishes a Smithsonian calendar of events on the third Friday of every month, and a Literary Calendar on the first or last Sunday of every month. The Air and Space Museum, National Gallery of Art, National Archives, Park Service, Kennedy Center, and Corcoran Gallery *all* publish free calendars.

If you are here to get some serious writing done, you will have ample opportunity to avoid it.

## Literary Landmarks

You have tramped all over Washington. After sitting on many a park bench wondering about what to do next, and staring at dozens of statues of generals on horseback, you need something new—you need *inspiration*.

Washington has inspired writers to write, given them refuge, and provided them with the means to write ever since it was founded. However, over the years, Washington has changed. In 1842, Charles Dickens wrote: "It is sometimes called the City of Magnificent Distances, but it might be with greater propriety the City of Magnificent Intentions, for it is only in taking a bird's eye view of it from the top of the Capitol that one can at all comprehend the vast designs of its projector, an aspiring Frenchman. Spacious avenues, that begin in nothing and lead no where; streets miles long that only want houses, roads, and inhabitants; public buildings that need but a public place to complete; and ornaments of great thoroughfares, which only lack great thoroughfares to ornament—are its leading features." There have been changes since then. Sources of inspiration have multiplied.

Start with the various allegorical figures. One group, *The Arts of Peace*, is near the entrance to Rock Creek Parkway. "Literature" carries a book and stands next to Pegasus. Ready to flee.

The largest collection of allegorical figures is at the main entrance to the Library of Congress. Two figures show "Composition" and "Reflection." See—it's official that you have to spend endless hours in reflection before you can compose. No one says you can't reflect while dancing, drinking, or reading mystery stories. The main doors to the Library show "Tradition," "Writing," and "Printing." However, you should not assume

# Writers' Bars

**The Class Reunion,** 1726 H Street, NW. Still a hangout for reporters, even following the departure of such Carter-era luminaries as Jody Powell and Hamilton Jordan.

**Herb's,** 2111 P Street, NW. A special table set aside for writers and occasional poetry readings make this bar/restaurant especially appealing.

**Jenkins Hill,** 223 Pennsylvania Avenue, SE. A favorite of the Capitol Hill press crowd.

**Kramer Books & Afterwords,** 1517 Connecticut Avenue, NW. Washington's first bookstore/cafe is one place where it's more than okay to read at the table.

**Millie & Al's,** 2440 18th Street, NW. The pride of Adams-Morgan; named "best neighborhood bar" by *Washingtonian* magazine.

**Trav's Inn,** 6119 Tulane Avenue, Glen Echo, Maryland. An old-fashioned roadhouse complete with jukebox, Trav's attracts writers and artists from the nearby Writer's Center and Glen Echo Park, as well as bikers and hikers from the C&O Canal towpath.

*—Thomazine Shanahan*

that these three topics are always related. Perhaps you can start a new "Tradition"—"Thinking About Writing a Lot" and "Storing What Is Written in a Trunk in the Attic."

As long as you are at the Library of Congress admiring the doors, go in and look at the Gutenberg Bible in the Great Hall. There *was* life before word processors.

The greatest monument to a writer in Washington is built to one who never visited here. The Folger Shakespeare Library has an extraordinary collection of works by and about Shakespeare and his world. The building is fascinating, with a wonderful theatre to see Shakespeare performed with class and style by a company that speaks the words with care. There is always an exhibit in the Great Hall, and you can study the panels around the outside of the building. The Puck Fountain, on the west end of the building, faces the Library of Congress and the Capitol. "What fools these mortals be."

There is an eclectic set of busts around the top of the Library of Congress. Goethe, Benjamin Franklin, Demosthenes, Washington Irving, Sir Walter Scott, Emerson, Macaulay, Hawthorne, and Dante. Ivanhoe, Faust, and Ichabod Crane. Curious.

There is a statue of Blackstone, who codified English law and inspired our Constitution. Go to the Archives and look at the original Constitution, Bill of Rights, and Declaration of Independence. Each concise, complete statements of a theme. Then visit the Jefferson Memorial, where the Declaration is edited to fit the architecture. This should be a reminder to writers everywhere. When you finish your life's work, try to be around to supervise when the world erects a monument in your honor.

Of course Washington writers don't always write of politics. Some poets and novelists lived here, while others just stopped by. And few of them left monuments behind. But—John Philip Sousa composed here, and is buried at Congressional Cemetery. John Howard Payne wrote many obscure plays. He was not a resident of Washington, but he is buried in Oak Hill Cemetery. A stanza of his "Home Sweet Home" is quoted on his memorial. Our most famous songwriter was Francis Scott Key, although he completed his masterpiece up the road in Baltimore. The flag that inspired him is hanging in the Smithsonian. He lived in Georgetown for 22 years in Key House, which was torn down in 1948. Part of Key Bridge is built on its grounds.

Washington periodically produces a "Washington Novel." The prototype (and perhaps still the best example) was *Democracy* by Henry Adams. Adams lived on Lafayette Square, in a house that was torn down in 1927 to make room for the Hay-Adams Hotel. The ground floor arches survived and were moved to 2618 31st Street, NW. In his *Education*, Adams described Washington in 1860: ". . . the same rude colony was camped in the same forest, with the same unfinished Greek temples for workrooms, and sloughs for roads. The Government had an air of social instability and incompleteness that went far to support the right of secession in theory as in fact; but right or wrong, secession was likely to be easy where there was so little to secede from." Adams considered Washington his home, and when his wife committed suicide in 1885, he commissioned Augustus Saint-Gaudens to design a monument to her. Saint-Gaudens called it "The Mystery of the Hereafter" and "The Peace of God that Passeth Understanding." Mark Twain referred to it as "Grief," and that is the name by which it is commonly known.

The entire memorial (the outdoor room in which it sits was designed by Stanford White) is in Rock Creek Cemetery. If that isn't convenient, go to the courtyard of the National Museum of American Art/National Portrait Gallery where there's a reproduction of the statue. It's an easy walk from the Archives.

The Portrait Gallery/American Art building was a hospital during the Civil War, and Walt Whitman worked there reading to patients and serving as a nurse. He described Washington in 1862: ". . . this is the greatest place of delays and puttings off, and not finding the clue to anything." Whitman spent quite a bit of time here, but the Portrait Gallery/American Art building is the only building he was associated with that remains standing. For instance, he lived in a boarding house at 1205 M Street, NW, but it was torn down to build a home for senior citizens. And it isn't even called the Whitman Arms.

The Portrait Gallery has paintings of many famous writers, and periodically presents "Portraits in Motion," a series of performances about the lives of people whose portraits are in the collection.

There are other poets associated with Washington. Paul Laurence Dunbar was born here. Paul Claudel was the French ambassador to Washington in the 1930s. Joaquin Miller wrote about the West, but lived for a time on Meridian Hill. Ruben Dario has a monument near the Pan American Union. There is a statue of Dante in Meridian Hill Park. And one of Longfellow on Connecticut Avenue. Elinor Wylie was from Washington, and she scandalized society by having an affair with a married Washington attorney. Inspiration for a traditional Washington novel?

Nathaniel Hawthorne visited here, staying at the Willard Hotel (the one before the one that now stands) where he noted that Washingtonians seemed to drink a lot: ". . . the conviviality of Washington sets in at an early hour and, so far as I had the opportunity to observe, never terminates at any hour. . . ." So if you feel the need for a drink after roaming about the city, you are part of a long-standing Washington tradition.

In 1877, Frederick Douglass said of Washington: "Wherever the American citizen may be a stranger, he is at home here." Cedar Hill, the home of Frederick Douglass, is still standing at 1411 W Street, SE and is open to the public. As chaplain of the

Senate, Edward Everett Hale (*The Man Without a Country*) lived at 1741 N Street, NW, in a house that is now part of the Tabard Inn. And Marjorie Kinnan Rawlings (*The Yearling*) grew up in a still-standing house at 1221 Newton Street, NE. Neither the Hale nor the Rawlings house is open to the public. And there is 1219 I Street, NW, where Frances Hodgson Burnett wrote *Little Lord Fauntleroy*. It's now a decrepit building next to a pornographic bookstore across from the bus station. So not only do you have to stay alive to make sure your memorial is correct—you also have to make sure that your home is maintained by the National Park Service.

The Hirshhorn Sculpture Garden has the imposing statue of Balzac by Rodin, as well as busts of T.S. Eliot, Bertrand Russell, Joseph Conrad, and Somerset Maugham.

All of these landmarks are in Washington. But one of the greatest American novelists is buried in Rockville. F. Scott Fitzgerald's father was from Montgomery County, and many ancestors were buried in the cemetery of St. Mary's Church. So Scott and Zelda are buried there, too. Two writers, right in the middle of Rockville. Their gravestone is engraved with the last line of *The Great Gatsby*: "So we beat on, boats against the current, borne back ceaselessly into the past."

Go home and read *Gatsby* (a real Literary Landmark) again.

# Index

## A

AFL-CIO, 41, 43
academic publishers, 118-120
Acropolis Books, 121
agents, literary, 124-125
Agriculture, Department of, 12
  Graduate School, 148-149,
  152-153
Agronsky & Kraft, 124
Alexander Laubert's Books, 140
*Almanac of American Politics*, 11,
  23
American Association for the
  Advancement of Science, 103
American Association of Retired
  Persons, 36
American Cafe, 165
American Chemical Society, 103
American Council of Education,
  95
American Film Institute, 58, 171
  as photo source, 78
American Medical Association,
  103
American Medical Writers
  Association, 87, 155
*American Educator*, 97
American Enterprise Institute, 23,
  45-46
American Retail Federation, 41
*American School Board Journal*,
  97
American Society of Association
  Executives, 31, 39, 40, 60, 90
American Society of Magazine
  Photographers, 79
American Society of Picture
  Professionals, 79
American Travel Writers, Society
  of, 157
American University, 144
  library, 65
Andrik Associates, 120
antiquarian and used books,
  140-141
Archives, National, *see* National
  Archives and Records Service
Archives of American Art, 56
Arena Stage, 78, 170
art galleries, 167, 168, 170, 177,
  178
Association Executives, American
  Society of, 31, 39, 40, 60, 90
Association of Science-Technology
  Centers, The, 103
association publishing, 122

associations, 31-35, 38-43, 95-98
  education, 95-98
  libraries, 58, 59, 60, 103
  and business writing, 89-90
Atomic Industrial Forum, 103

## B

Backstage Inc., 136
bars, writers', 175
bathrooms, best 165
Bed and Breakfast League Ltd.,
  172
Bob's Famous ice cream, 165
Book Annex, The, 136-137
Book Cellar, The, 140
Book Ends, 140
book packaging, 121
book publishers, 118-125
book publishing courses, 151-152
books
  on government, 22-23
  on libraries, 54
  on lobbying, 44
Booked Up, 140
Bookhouse, 140
bookstores, 135-141
  used, 140-141
Brookings Institution, 45
BSW Literary Agency Inc., 124
Buchwald, Ann, 124
Bureau of Labor Statistics, 13, 90
  *See also* Labor, Department of.
Bureau of Land Management, 13
Bureau of National Affairs, 119
Bureau of the Census, 12, 60
Business Roundtable, 41, 42
business, small, 108-109
business writing, 88-93

## C

Cabinet offices, *see* executive
  branch, or specific agency name.
Capitol Hill
  federal government and, 89,
  90-91
  industry groups and, 89-90
  special interest publications
  and, 90-91
  Washington industries and,
  92-93
  *See also* Congress.